ON KNOWING REALITY

Ārya Asaṅga (Tib. Thogs-med), the "Unhindered One," depicted here in his dialectical, debate posture. From a Tibetan woodblock print.

ON KNOWING REALITY

The *Tattvārtha* Chapter of Asaṅga's *Bodhisattvabhūmi*

Translated with
Introduction,
Commentary, and Notes
by
JANICE DEAN WILLIS

NEW YORK
COLUMBIA UNIVERSITY PRESS
1979

Library of Congress Cataloging in Publication Data

Asaṅga.

On knowing reality.

Translation of Tattvārthapaṭala, the 4th chapter of pt. 1 of Bodhisattvabhūmi, the 15th section of Yogācārabhūmi.

Bibliography: p.

1. Yogācāra (Buddhism) I. Willis, Janice Dean. II. Title.

BQ3062.E54W54 1979 294.3'4'2 79-16047

ISBN 0-231-04604-9

Columbia University Press
New York Guildford, Surrey

Printed in the United States of America

To Professor Alex Wayman
and to My Parents

Contents

Preface *ix*
Introduction *1*
History of the Text and the Life of Its Author *3*
The Yogācāra School of the Māhāyana *13*
Two Threads of the Yogācāra and Some Later Confusions *20*
Contents of the Chapter *37*
Notes to the Introduction *47*
The Chapter on Knowing Reality *67*
The Chapter on Knowing Reality: Running Translation *147*
Glossary *177*
Selected Bibliography *193*

Preface

The *Tattvārtha-paṭalam,* or the Chapter on Knowing Reality, forms the fourth chapter of Part I of the illustrious text, the *Bodhisattvabhūmi,* composed in the late fourth century by the renowned Buddhist sage and philosopher, Ārya Asaṅga. The text was written in Sanskrit and, having acquired immediate success and fame as a Mahāyāna scripture in its own right, was quickly translated into Chinese and subsequently into Tibetan.

In many respects, the *Tattvārtha* chapter is the focal point of the entire treatise. It is the only chapter which addresses itself specifically to Mahāyāna doctrine, laying bare for the reader the proper ways in which reality should be understood and perceived by one coursing in the Bodhisattva Vehicle. By doing so, it directly takes up the central concern of all Buddhist doctrine, namely, the epistemological concern of correctly judging and validating knowledge about reality as it really is.

Now that the present translation of the chapter is available, Asaṅga's place of esteem among the classical Buddhist doctors is clearly illustrated. Its exposition also greatly clarifies Asaṅga's actual position with respect to Mahāyāna doctrine, which until now has been frequently misconstrued by contemporary Buddhologists.

It is truly remarkable that in this "Dharma-ending age" such a clear explication of the proper modes of cognizing reality according to Buddhist doctrine is now available to us, after almost sixteen hundred years. Existing only in Sanskrit, Tibetan, and Chinese editions, the text has for many centuries been unavailable to Western readers, even though the whole of the *Bodhisattvabhūmi* enjoyed immediate success following its original composition. It was translated into Chinese in the early fifth century by the Chinese savant, Dharmakṣema, and some time later, into Tibetan by the sage-translator Prajñāvarman. However, until the present work there has been no complete translation of the *Tattvārtha* chapter into any Western language.

My work with this text, as well as with Asaṅga's own exegesis of the chapter and other pertinent texts, served as part of the subject of my Ph.D. dissertation work at Columbia University. Having completed the doctorate there, I felt it appropriate and opportune to attempt to make this classic treatise available to a larger group of interested readers. What follows represents the fruit of this effort.

Many people offered their kind and invaluable assistance as I worked on the early phases of this project. My gratitude is extended to Prof. M. Nagatomi, who kindly took two days off from his busy schedule to introduce me to the use of Harvard University's Tibetan collection. During a few weeks' stay in Kathmandu, Nepal in 1974, Mr. Nyingma Lama offered clear explication with regard to some of the more difficult passages of the chapter. His illuminating examples were useful as I settled into the work of translating the chapter itself.

It was my good fortune to spend a month in Madison, Wisconsin the following year, making use of the university's Buddhist Studies collection. In addition, the personal library of the late Professor Richard Robinson was generously placed at my disposal. Most importantly, Geshe Lhundup Sopa revealed to me his broad and deep mastery of Buddhist philosophy, particularly assisting me in the translation of Asaṅga's very terse and abstruse commentary on the chapter. As this exegetical text is a "root commentary," its meaning could have been fully developed only by one such as he, thoroughly versed in the tradition. My thanks to him are limitless. Responsible for arranging my stay in Wisconsin was my *kalyāṇamitra* of seven years, Lama Thubten Yeshe, a teacher of the Gelugpa tradition, whose incisive wisdom is matched only by his all-encompassing compassion.

Valued as teacher and guide was Professor Alex Wayman of Columbia University. It was he who first suggested that I attempt the project, and who painstakingly reviewed it at every phase. I thank him earnestly for introducing me to the profound depths of Buddhist studies and the illustrious writings of Ārya Asaṅga. Without his guidance, the thesis work would not have been brought to fruition.

It should be mentioned however that this book is not, in any direct sense, solely a revision of the dissertation. Much of the technical discussion found there has been left out here, replaced by a more general introduction to the materials. Asaṅga's detailed exegesis of the work, parts of which were translated in full for the dissertation, finds only mention here; while the "commentary" found here was completely absent from the dissertation. Thus there has been a rather complete reorganization of materials, the benefits of which only time will judge.

My long-time friend, Randa Solick, deserves deep thanks, not only for typing the many drafts of the work, but for offering continued encouragement and support as I read and re-read Asaṅga's works. Robert Solick, a student of psychology as well as Buddhist doctrine, likewise deserves my gratitude for his helpful suggestions as the work progressed, as well as for assisting me with the early preparation of the glossary. Ms. Louise Gross typed and retyped manuscript copy. I am grateful for her tireless help.

My sincere appreciation must be offered to Professor Robert Thurman of Amherst College for his careful reading and invaluable critique of the draft manuscript of this work. The book's present form is due in large measure to his helpful suggestions and, without them, should no doubt be the worse for it. In this regard I must also offer thanks to Ms. Karen Mitchell, editor of the manuscript for Columbia University Press. Whatever smoothness and clarity of expression is found here is due to her painstaking editing. I gratefully acknowledge her patient, dedicated, and extremely insightful suggestions.

A word about the translation of the chapter and its presentation here may prove helpful to the reader. For the most part, I have tried to give as literal a translation of the text as possible, while remaining cognizant of the fact that the English and Sanskrit idioms are not perfectly matched. Some English expressions have been added for the sake of clarity, but at no point, I trust, have such additions served to distort the meaning of the original Sanskrit.

The information given in the commentary is primarily drawn from two sources: (1) my own understanding of the text as it stands in its own right and in the light of the history of Buddhist thought in general; and (2) the critically important and informative exegesis of the chapter written by Asaṅga.

I have provided a running translation of the text without commentary so that readers interested in reading straight through the translation without interruption may do so. This is followed by a glossary and a selected bibliography. The notes to the "Introduction" include material intended primarily for the specialist, but should also inform the interested general reader.

In order to produce this translation, I read the Sanskrit and Tibetan texts side by side, after having first read each edition through separately. For the Sanskrit version of the chapter, I read both Wogihara's and Dutt's editions of the text, but have relied most closely on the edition by Dutt. The Tibetan edition used is that found in the *Tibetan Tripiṭaka,* Peking edition *(PTT).*

I consulted two "pada" commentaries in their extant Tibetan editions: one by Guṇaprabha, the *Bodhisattvabhūmivṛtti,* and the other by Sāgaramegha, the *Yogācārya-bhūmau bodhisattvabhūmi vyākhyā,* at the urging of the traditional Tibetan sources. However, neither of these "pada" commentaries added additional insights into the chapter's key ideas. Presumably, both Guṇaprabha and Sāgaramegha wrote their commentaries on the *Tattvārtha* chapter for completeness' sake, both being mainly interested in other chapters of the *Bodhisattvahūmi,* notably its *Śīla* chapter. Asaṅga's own exegesis of the chapter, as could be expected, was the most helpful in expounding the chapter's essential aspects. His exegesis was read in the Tibetan edition found in *PTT.* Of course, contemporary translations of certain key scriptures associated with the Yogācāra and other secondary materials have also informed my work. A selected bibliography of these and other important works can be found at the end of this book.

My early work was generously supported by grants from the Danforth Foundation and the University of California's Steinhart Fellowship and greatly facilitated by the understanding and cooperation of Provost Herman Blake of Oakes College, the University of California at Santa Cruz.

Lastly, I wish to express my deepest thanks to Professor Barbara Stoler Miller, of Barnard College and Columbia University, who encouraged me to revise the manuscript for publication. Of course, it should go without saying that whatever oversights or errors still remain in the work are due solely to my own imperfections.

Janice Dean Willis
Santa Cruz, California

Introduction

History of the Text and the Life of Its Author

The news spread everywhere that the Mahāyāna, which once declined, was again spread in all directions.
—Tāranātha, *History of Buddhism in India.*

Asaṅga's encyclopedic *Yogācārabhūmi,*[1] composed in the late 4th century A.D., is comprised of five major divisions.[2] The first division, called the *Bahubhūmikavastu* (The Division of Many Stages), expounds the Buddhist doctrine in seventeen separate volumes,[3] each entitled *bhūmi* or "stage." The fifteenth such volume, the *Bodhisattvabhūmi,* enjoyed immediate success and fame in its own right, and has always been regarded with special reverence as a Mahāyāna text. While other works of Asaṅga, and later of his half-brother Vasubandhu, were transmitted into China at a much later date,[4] the sage Dharmakṣema saw it proper to translate the *Bodhisattvabhūmi* into Chinese in 418 A.D.,[5] very soon after its composition.

In the Tibetan tradition, Asaṅga's *Bodhisattvabhūmi* was counted as one of the six basic texts of the *bka' gdams pa* school founded by Atīśa (which later became the reformed *dGe lugs pa* sect under Tsoṅ-kha-pa).[6] Bu-ston's *History,* which often quotes directly from this text, lists it as one of the "treatises conducive to Salvation and Omniscience."[7] Indeed, since its composition the *Bodhisattvabhūmi* has remained a standard textbook in all Mahāyāna monastic institutions. It is considered essential reading for gaining an understanding of the proper ways in which a bodhisattva ("one intent on obtaining *bodhi,* or enlightenment") should conduct himself, meditate, and understand the Buddha's teaching. "The Chapter on Knowing Reality" *(Tattvārtha-paṭalam),* the fourth chapter of Part I of the *Bodhisattvabhūmi* (along with Asaṅga's exegesis of the chapter, found in his *Viniścayasaṃgrahaṇī*)[8] is central to the text of the *Bodhisattvabhūmi* as a whole, and is aimed solely at instructing one coursing in the bodhisattva vehicle in the correct ways in which to perceive reality, according to the Buddha's doctrine.

According to all traditional scriptures, the author of these texts, Asaṅga, attained the rank of a third-stage bodhisattva.[9] The name assigned to one of this stage is *Prabhākarī,* "Light-giving" or "Illuminating,"[10] since that bodhisattva "diffuses the great light of the Doctrine among the living beings."[11] In this stage his thoughts are "pure, constant, unworldly, dispassionate, firm, resolute, ardent, ambitious, noble and magnanimous."[12] He longs only for Buddha-knowledge, devotes himself night and day to studying the scriptures, to self-examination and meditation. Such a bodhisattva "attains to all the higher stages of meditation, enters into the sublime abodes, sports in the stations freed of limitations, and perfects the supernatural faculties."[13] He rids himself of sensuous desire, of ignorance, and of metaphysical speculation. He practices supreme patience *(kṣānti)* and is solely intent on promoting the good of others. And as such is Asaṅga, the Ārya and "master practitioner of yoga" (the true Yogācārya) revered by Mahāyāna adherents.

The specific details of Asaṅga's life are elusive, because most of the sources are legendary accounts.[14] This is not surprising, since it is not unusual to find the lives of great Buddhist sages embellished in such ways—as was the life of Gautama Buddha himself. The most well-known narratives of the Ārya's life are found in Bu-ston's and Tāranātha's legend-like histories. The account given by Paramārtha is the most authoritative historical source, though that account addresses itself mainly to the biography of Vasubandhu.[15] The approximate dates of Asaṅga's life can be deduced from a study of his works. He was probably born during the latter half of the fourth century A.D. and he died sometime before the mid-fifth century.[16]

According to the account given by Tāranātha,[17] Asaṅga's mother, in a previous incarnation, had been a learned Buddhist monk pledged to Avalokiteśvara, who was his tutelary deity. Because that monk had once "deeply wounded the sentiments"[18] of another monk while debating with him, Avalokiteśvara predicted that he would be reborn repeatedly as a woman. During one such rebirth, as a woman named Prasannaśīlā,[19] the life of Ārya Asaṅga begins.

Prasannaśīlā, recognizing the great misfortunes that had befallen Buddhism in India,[20] prayed to Lord Avalokita to be of aid to the Dharma. As a result of her prayers, three sons were born to her, all of whom later joined the Buddhist order. Apparently, Prasannaśīlā was a brahman woman of the Kauśika clan. According to all accounts, she gave birth to Asaṅga first, after her union with a kṣatriya man. She later gave birth to two other sons, these times through union with a brahman. All accounts agree that Asaṅga was the eldest of the three brothers; Vasubandhu was second, and Viriñcivatsa was last.[21] The family resided in the Gāndhāra region at Puruṣapura, modern-day Peshawar.

Some sources say that Asaṅga was born with auspicious signs,[22] and that, even as a child, he went to forest groves away from his home and meditated on teachings received from a tantric sage by the name of Jetari. At home his mother instructed him in writing, debate, arithmetic, medicine, fine arts, and the like, and he became highly proficient in all of these.

At an early age he went for ordination as a Buddhist monk. He humbly and devotedly served the saṅgha and was apparently a child of amazingly quick intelligence. It is said that "every year, he memorized a hundred thousand śloka-s and grasped their significance."[23] Paramārtha tells us that all three sons initially became Sarvāstivādins,[24] placing them within the Hīnayāna tradition. Though this was probably true for Asaṅga, who entered monastic life much earlier than his half-brothers, there is clear evidence that before entering the Mahāyāna he belonged for many years to the sect known as the later Mahīśāsakas.[25] Along with their unique blue vestments, the Mahīśāsakas were famed for the great emphasis the sect placed upon meditation.[26] Such early training was to leave a profound and lasting impression upon Asaṅga.

Under a teacher named Piṇḍola,[27] who is referred to in Paramārtha's history as an arhat, Asaṅga studied assiduously. He learned all the sūtras, mastered the Hīnayāna scriptures, and read many of the Mahāyāna texts.[28] When he took up the study of the *Prajñāpāramitā-sūtras,* he had difficulties in obtaining a clear understanding of them and begged guidance from his guru. Apparently, it was then that he took a certain initiation *(abhiṣeka)*[29] and set out to obtain clear instruction directly from his tutelary deity, Lord Maitreya Buddha.

Here begins the most famous chapter in the life of the Ārya. Asaṅga, having taken leave of his guru, retreated to a cave on a mountain referred to in the scriptures as Kukkuṭapāda.[30] There he was to remain in solitary and silent meditative search for twelve long, arduous years. The annals of Bu-ston and Tāranātha go into some detail regarding this twelve-year period. It is said that Asaṅga initially propitiated Lord Maitreya for three years, but having seen no signs of success in his practice, he became disheartened and came out of the cave. Shortly after venturing outside, he noticed some stones that had been worn down solely by the wings of birds as they made their daily flights to and from their nests in the rocks. Thinking to himself "So, I have lost assiduity,"[31] he reentered his cave and began his practice once more.

Again, after three more years of meditating, he became once more disheartened and left his retreat. This time, he noticed some stones that had been eroded by single drops of water; and with renewed vigor, he entered again into solitary practice.

Likewise, another three years elapsed with still no signs of success. He determined to give up his practice and again left his cave. After journeying some distance from the cave, he came across an old man "rubbing a piece of iron with soft cotton and saying, 'I am going to prepare fine needles out of this.' "[32] Then the man showed to Asaṅga needles he had already made in such a manner. Asaṅga returned to his retreat.

Again three more years elapsed, bringing his tenure in the meditation cave to twelve years in all, but no signs of success appeared. Utterly disappointed, Asaṅga decided to abandon his practice completely. He left his cave and journeyed far away.

On the outskirts of a town, he came upon a dog, the lower part of its body eaten by worms. Seeing this, Asaṅga became filled with compassion. He thought to himself, "To remove the worms would destroy them, but if they are not removed, the dog will die." On that spot he resolved to cut flesh from his own body and attract the worms to it. Accordingly he went into the town, called Acinta,[33] and trading his mendicant's staff, obtained a golden knife. Then he returned to the place where the dog lay infested and proceeded to cut the flesh from his own thigh. He then decided that if he took up the worms with his hands they would nevertheless perish. So, closing his eyes, he determined to transport them to his own flesh by using his tongue. At just that moment the dog disappeared and, in its place, Asaṅga beheld the Lord Maitreya, full of light.[34] With tears flowing from his eyes, Asaṅga asked,

> "Oh my father, my unique refuge,
> I have exerted myself in a hundred different ways,
> But nevertheless no result was to be seen.
> Wherefore have the rain-clouds and the might of the ocean,
> Come only now, when, tormented by violent pain,
> I am no longer thirsting?"

Maitreya answered,

> "Though the king of the gods sends down rain,
> A bad seed is unable to grow.
> Though the Buddhas may appear [in this world]
> He who is unworthy cannot partake of the bliss."[35]

Maitreya then informed Asaṅga that he had been present near him from the very beginning but because of Asaṅga's own mental obstructions, he had been unable to see him. Now, after practicing with such fervor and finally balancing that with such great compassion, Asaṅga was capable of beholding him. Then Maitreya instructed Asaṅga to lift him up and carry him into the town upon his shoulders. Asaṅga did so. But Lord Maitreya could not be perceived by anyone but Asaṅga.[36] The Ārya then believed the great events which had taken place and entered immediately into the *srotaḥ-anugata-nāma-samādhi,* the samādhi called the "stream of faith."

Lord Maitreya, full of light, then inquired of Asaṅga what it was that he wished of him. Asaṅga replied, "I am searching for instructions on how to spread the Mahāyāna doctrine."[37] It was at this point that Maitreya told Asaṅga to take hold of the corner of his robe, and in that very moment, Asaṅga was transported to the Tuṣita heaven[38] of the Lord Maitreya himself.

There are various accounts of the length of time Asaṅga spent in Tuṣita. Some reports mention six months, while others mention fifty-three years.[39] Whatever the period of stay, it was apparently during this time that Asaṅga listened to Maitreya expound the Mahāyāna doctrine in its entirety and that he learned the real significance of all the sūtras. Having accomplished this, Asaṅga then listened to the "Five Books"[40] of Maitreya. As before, it is said that Asaṅga immediately attained samādhi on each aspect of the teachings.

The events describing Asaṅga's meditative search for and his subsequent meeting with Maitreya are referred to in the Tibetan tradition as *rnam thar,* that is, biographical details which serve as guides for later readers' "complete liberation" *(rnam par thar pa).* A special genre of religious literature, *rnam thar* may be described as "sacred biography," concerned with unfolding for the reader the inner "spiritual" development of the particular sage discussed, and thereby, the very path to Buddhahood. Hence, though such details may read as legend, they are considered essential to the heart of Dharma practice.

When all these studies with the Lord were completed, Asaṅga returned to the human realm, and straight away set to work for the welfare of all beings. From this time onward the name Maitreyanātha ("one devoted to Maitreya") becomes an epithet associated with Asaṅga and his written works.

Having successfully completed his meditations and studies with Maitreya, Asaṅga was fully equipped to work for the good of mankind. As he had attained a mastery of the *abhijñās* (supernormal faculties obtained through meditation), he is said to have been able to "know the minds of others" *(paracitta-abhijñā),* as well as to employ other extrasensory powers. All these accomplishments greatly enhanced his ability to spread the Mahāyāna doctrine effectively.

Apparently, Asaṅga's first acts were to establish several monastic abodes, or *vihāras,* after having attracted monks through his authoritative explanations of the Dharma. It was in one such vihāra, later known as the Dharmāṅkura-vihāra (the "monastery from which the Dharma again sprouted")[41] that Asaṅga set down in writing his profound understanding of the Buddha's teaching. First, with the help of students, he put into written form the "Five Books" of Maitreya.[42] Then he settled in to composing his own treatises. The first of these was a brief "compendium" of the Abhidharma, in a work entitled the *Abhidharmasamuccaya.*[43] This work was probably followed by his "summary" of Mahāyāna practice, the *Mahāyānasaṃgraha.*[44] It was also during this time that he produced his commentary on the *Prajñāpāramitā* texts.[45] Next he began the mammoth work for which he is best known: the *Yogācārabhūmi,* or "The Stages of Practice of [Buddhist] Yoga." When he had completed the *Bodhisattvabhūmi* volume of this work, his fame as a master expounder of the Mahāyāna spread far and wide.

As he completed these major treatises, Asaṅga continued to instruct a great many *śrāvakas* ("Hearers," monks of the

Hīnayāna tradition) in the doctrine of the Mahāyāna. Because of his great erudition, he came to the attention of a king named Gambhīrapakṣa.[46] That king became the Ārya's royal patron, and with his aid Asaṅga founded many new monasteries. So the Mahāyāna once again took root and flowered in India.

It is said that though the Mahāyāna had long before spread in India, prior to Asaṅga's preaching it had greatly declined. Some of the monks could recite Mahāyāna sūtras but without understanding their meaning. Tāranātha's account says that "even during the time of the most extensive spread of the Mahāyāna, the number of the Mahāyāna monks did not reach ten thousand"[47] and that "even in the days of Nāgārjuna, most of the monks were *śrāvaka*-s."[48] But owing to the Ārya's teaching and writings, during his own lifetime the number of Mahāyāna monks reached "tens of thousands."[49] Thus is Asaṅga revered as the foremost expounder of the Mahāyāna doctrine and as the compassionate cause of its rejuvenation.

During all the rest of his years, Asaṅga never tired of studying and teaching the Buddha's Dharma. Some years after he had completed his compositions, he converted his younger half-brother Vasubandhu to the Mahāyāna and adopted him as a student.[50] In connection with this conversion, it is interesting to note that Vasubandhu, even as a śrāvaka, had never been associated with the Mahīśāsaka sect that Asaṅga had belonged to. Rather than focus on the meditative life, Vasubandhu had always devoted himself to Buddhist philosophy and dialectics. At an early age he had gone to Kashmir to study with Saṅghabhadra, a teacher renowned for his erudition especially with regard to the scriptures of the Hīnayāna.[51] Here he was successful in mastering the three *Śrāvaka-piṭakas* and became proficient in the *Vi-*

bhāṣa,[52] the philosophical scriptures of the so-called eighteen Buddhist schools.

Moreover, tradition holds that Vasubandhu, in each of his five hundred previous births, had always been a pandit and one drawn to philosophical speculation.[53] Consequently, while Vasubandhu remained a devout student of Buddhist philosophy, his older brother was always firmly centered in the direct experience of the Buddha's Dharma. The Ārya eventually was successful in converting his half-brother to the Mahāyāna and so taught the doctrine to him as well as to other disciples. Later, following Asaṅga's death, it was Vasubandhu who became the "popularizer" of the Ārya's teachings.

After writing many important works, erecting numerous vihāras, and instructing countless monks in the true understanding of the Mahāyāna doctrine, Ārya Asaṅga, the "Light-Giving One," passed away in the city of Rājagṛha.[54] There his disciples built a caitya with his relics.

The Yogācāra School of the Mahāyāna

I have mentioned Asaṅga's important work of building vihāras, writing numerous treatises, and instructing countless monk disciples—all of which was instrumental in reviving the Mahāyāna. But history remembers him chiefly for his role as founder of a new school of Mahāyāna Buddhism, the Yogācāra. As the name implies, Asaṅga's school continued to emphasize meditation and the practice of yoga *(yogācāra)* as central to the realization of *bodhi* or enlightenment.[55] Later, this school underwent certain changes, becoming known first as the *Vijñānavāda* (the so-called "consciousness-only" school) and then, the *Vijñaptimātratāvāda* (the "representation-only" school), owing to the popularization of Asaṅga's teaching through the independent works of Vasubandhu and later doctors of the lineage.

Modern-day Buddhist scholars almost unanimously characterize the Yogācāra as being a school of Buddhist idealism, but to view it solely in this way distorts the true sense of Asaṅga's teaching. Asaṅga's works were aimed at correcting the mistaken views held by many Buddhist adherents of his day concerning the true meaning of the Mahāyāna scriptures. To be sure, the single, most misunderstood doctrine taught by these texts was that of *śūnyatā,* "voidness" or "emptiness."

Śūnyatā as "emptiness" points to the absence of intrinsic

reality, of an abiding self or essence in all phenomena of the relative world, whether of persons or things. Persons and things are in truth devoid of self and devoid of essence. *Śūnyatā* does not mean nothingness, however, but that no thing exists of its own, in its own right.

The doctrine of śūnyatā was not a new creation of the Mahāyāna[56]—having been mentioned in many of the discourses of the Buddha himself—but it became central in the *Prajñāpāramitā* literature and was explicated most forcefully by the great Mahāyāna thinker Nāgārjuna,[57] who lived some two hundred years before Asaṅga. Nāgārjuna founded the other great wing of the Mahāyāna, the school of the Mādhyamika, which taught the "Middle Path." Nāgārjuna remains revered for his pristine wisdom and for his precise and cutting intellect. His critical explication of śūnyatā was searing. For many, it was devastating. As a result of his thoroughgoing critical philosophy, many came to misinterpret śūnyatā as a doctrine of rank nihilism and to fear it. It was this troubled situation within the Buddhist community that Asaṅga inherited. He sought to set things aright by explaining śūnyatā in a more positive way.

Before going further it may prove helpful here to briefly review the historical phases of Buddhist philosophy. Mahāyāna Buddhism recognizes three "Turnings of the Wheel of the Dharma,"[58] a phrase used to refer to the three divisions of the scripture, namely: (1) the early scriptures of the Hīnayāna[59] vehicle; (2) the intermediate scripture, which includes the *Prajñāpāramitā* literature and the Mādhyamika doctrine; and (3) the latest scripture, that of the Yogācāra doctrine. Some modern-day Buddhologists, using a sort of philosophical shorthand, have preferred to speak of these phases as those of (1) naïve realism, (2) criticism, and (3) idealism.[60] By such terminology they refer to successive philosophical periods, namely, of the radical pluralism of the early Hīnayāna dharma theory, the dialectical criticism of the Mādhyamika in response to the message of the *Prajñāpāramitā* texts, and the so-called absolutist idealism of the Yogācāra. Both the Mādhyamika of Nāgārjuna and the Yogācāra of Asaṅga were outgrowths of and responses to the *Prajñāpāramitā* literature's teaching on śūnyatā. Indeed, these two schools, which comprise the Mahāyāna, arose to clarify the *Prajñāpāramitā*'s message.

It has been generally assumed that the Mādhyamika and the Yogācāra are antithetical to each other, and scholars have sometimes pondered over the ordering of the "three turnings." How and why, some have queried, could the phase of idealism follow that of the rigorously critical philosophy of the Mādhyamika?[61] The present translation of the Reality Chapter should now make clear that, far from advocating idealism in an absolute sense, Asaṅga's statements here are intended to vindicate, expand upon, and clarify the fundamental notion of all Mahāyāna philosophy, i.e., śūnyatā itself. We can now see that Asaṅga, in fact, inherited the earlier realism of the Hīnayāna as well as the Mādhyamika's critical exposition of śūnyatā, and how—as a Mahāyānist philosopher and master meditator—he reformulated the explication of that doctrine. As more and more texts become available, in the original and in translation, the practice of dichotomizing the philosophical productions of the Mahāyāna according to whether a school is strictly concerned with emptiness or with idealism will hopefully lessen.[62] I will take up this issue again in the next section, but for the time being, a bit more concentration on the "three turnings" may prove valuable.

One might imagine the three as representing those stages of philosophical development within Buddhism which took as their respective metaphysical foci: (1) things (and here is meant *dharma* in its broadest sense, as any phenomenon, fact, or event that can be perceived, known, or thought to have a separate existence, as enumerated according to the Hīnayāna dharma theory); followed by (2) a consuming interest in *śūnyatā* as the denial of thing-ness (i.e. *dharmanairātmya,* the theory of the "non-self" of dharmas, particularly as articulated in the earliest Mahāyāna literature, the *Prajñāpāramitā);* and lastly (3) the *identification* of these two, that is, the identification of things and voidness.[63]

With the identification of dharmas and śūnyatā one realizes directly *dharmanairātmya,* the voidness of self-nature of all things. Now this realization is none other than that suggested repeatedly by the *Prajñāpāramitā* literature. It is posited explicitly by the *Heart Sutra: iha Śariputra rūpaṃ śūnyatā śūnyataiva rūpaṃ* ("Here, O Śariputra, form is voidness and voidness is form"). The transition in consciousness has progressed from the awareness of things in the first stage, to śūnyatā in the second, to finally an understanding of the two as "*not*-two." *Rūpaṃ eva śūnyaṃ.* Form is voidness and, vice-versa, that very voidness is form. The two cannot be found—indeed are not possible—as separate, individual entities.[64]

As I noted earlier, the *Prajñāpāramitā* literature served as the root sources for both Nāgārjuna and Asaṅga.[65] But the two thinkers chose different approaches, of language and of style, to elucidate the real meaning of śūnyatā. Nāgārjuna's negative and critical method frightened many, seeming to leave no ground on which to stand, let alone practice the Buddha's teaching. Nāgārjuna himself recognized the possibilities of misinterpretation. In his *Mūlamādhyamakakārikā* he quotes a possible objector: "If all this were void, then there would be no creation and no destruction. . . ." But confident in his understanding of voidness, Nāgārjuna replies, "If all this were *not* void, then there would be no creation and no destruction. . . ." Here he clearly gives expression to the fact that voidness is *not* nothingness. Rather, it is the necessary condition for there being anything at all. In keeping with the Middle Path (which thereby avoids the extremes of eternalism and nihilism), Nāgārjuna warned on the one hand against holding on to śūnyatā as though it were itself a hypostatized thing and, on the other, against believing that it meant the utter destruction of all reality. Unfortunately, however, Nāgārjuna's negative approach resulted in many followers' misinterpreting śūnyatā as unqualified nihilism. It was largely to correct this misunderstanding of the meaning of śūnyatā that Asaṅga wrote his philosophical works, a key representation of which is the *Tattva* chapter.[66]

In order to accomplish the task of clarifying the chief Mahāyāna doctrine in a balanced, intelligible, and less frightening way, Asaṅga employed a number of methods *(upāya)*. One was the invention of an "ontological psychological"[67] model for explaining the bifurcation of apparent reality into a subject and an object. More will be said about this model in the next section. Another was what might be called a nominalist approach. This approach figures prominently in the *Tattva* chapter. Yet another was the extremely important introduction of a new schema in which the model of the so-called "three natures" *(trisvabhāvas* or *trilakṣaṇa)* is used to extend and supplement the older Mahāyāna formula of the "two truths."

According to the older schema, a theory found in many early Mahāyāna texts and one of special importance to the Mādhyamika, reality or truth *(satya)* is comprised of two parts: (1) what might be called superficial, conventional, or relative reality, *saṃvṛti satya;* and (2) profound, ultimate, or absolute reality, *pāramārtha satya.* Thus the Mādhyamikas often supplied the qualifying word "ultimately" in contexts calling for an explanation of the way things are in truth in contradistinction to the way they seem.

For Asaṅga the two-truths theory was insufficient. He therefore devised a schema which states that all phenomena have three natures: (1) a mentally constructed and therefore imaginary *(parikalpita)* nature; (2) a dependent, or relative *(paratantra)* nature; and (3) a perfected or absolute *(pariniṣpanna)* nature. Employing this schema Asaṅga could go on to say—as Robert Thurman has succinctly summarized—that

> when all things are said to be empty of intrinsic substance, this only applies to them in their mentally constructed nature—they continue to exist as relative things, and their ineffable relativity devoid of conceptual differentiation is their absolute nature.[68]

The *parikalpita* nature of Asaṅga's schema is synonymous with the *saṃvṛti satya* of the two-truths theory and the *pariniṣpanna* is the ineffable correlate to *pāramārtha satya.* What Asaṅga has done by introducing a third category into the schema is to provide the Buddhist practitioner with *insulation* against nihilism.[69] He has accounted for the practical passage to liberation by providing for the transition in awareness from conventional to absolute knowing. He has affirmed śūnyatā as the *positive,* existent underlying principle and formal *structure* of all relative existence. In a passage from the *Tattva* chapter, Asaṅga writes:

> Now, how is voidness rightly conceptualized? Wherever and in whatever place something is not, one rightly observes that [place] to

be void of that [thing]. Moreover, whatever remains in that place one knows as it really is, that "here there is an existent."[70]

When all false dualities, of subject and object, of designations and bases of designations, are abandoned, voidness—as the *ultimate mode* of all relative existence—remains. As will be seen, Asaṅga's *Tattva* chapter speaks at length about the relationship between names *(prajñapti)* and their referents (here, *vastu),* and his exegesis of the chapter is firmly based on the schema of the three natures. The so-called "ontological-psychological" model which is most often associated with claims that the Yogācāra propounds a form of absolutist idealism is completely absent from these two texts. There is, however, reference to this model in the next section.

Two Threads of the Yogācāra and Some Later Confusions

If, as I have argued, Asaṅga's main concern in the *Tattva* chapter is to clarify the doctrine of śūnyatā, why is it that the school he founded is viewed—almost unanimously—as solely advocating an absolutist idealism? Part of the reason was noted by Dr. D. T. Suzuki when he wrote, in 1930:

> Most Buddhist scholars are often too ready to make a sharp distinction between the Mādhyamika and the Yogācāra school, taking the one as exclusively advocating the theory of emptiness *(śūnyatā)* while the other is bent singlemindedly on an idealistic interpretation of the universe. They thus further assume that the idea of emptiness is not at all traceable in the Yogācāra and that idealism is absent in the Mādhyamika. This is not exact as a matter of historical fact.[71]

In fact, several factors account for the erroneous perception of Asaṅga's actual position. There has seemed to be a tendency on the part of Buddhist scholars to treat the respective "schools" of Buddhism as rigidly advocating and adhering to singly defined positions, and to view the schools' founders as thinkers putting forth their own unique systems of thought in contradiction with each other and even with the canonical Buddhist texts.[72] To be sure, the classical

Buddhist doctors differed in style, understanding, and interpretive skill; yet to view them as antagonists because of this is misleading. The practice of treating the "schools" as discrete and inflexible units of philosophical doctrine promotes the view that they were antithetical to each other and that no continuity or sharing existed between them.

This seems clearly to have been the historical fate of the Yogācāra school, for scholars have consistently maintained that this school propounds idealism; that its central teaching is that "mind *(citta)* or consciousness *(vijñāna)* is the sole, or only *(mātra)*, reality."[73] Again, given the fact that—at least in the *Tattva* chapter—Asaṅga clearly posits *voidness,* not mind, as the only absolute in the final analysis, how is it that this remains the generally accepted assessment of the Yogācāra?

Assessments which claim to characterize the whole of Yogācāra thought as being uniformly "idealistic" take little notice of the fact that historically—and according to the texts themselves—there existed at least two varying streams of Yogācāra thought,[74] viz., (1) what may be called an "original" thread propounded by Maitreya, Asaṅga, Vasubandhu, and Sthiramati; and (2) a "later" thread which found expression notably through such doctors as Dharmapāla and Hsüan-tsang. Both "streams" were introduced into China—the earlier by Paramārtha and the later by Hsüan-tsang—and afterward transmitted also to Japan. Moreover, while there is clear evidence that the later stream of thought, as expounded by Dharmapāla and others, is "idealistic" in character,[75] the same cannot and should not be assumed for the earlier "thread," though, in fact, this has been generally the case.

A few recent comparative studies have shown that fundamental differences exist between the philosophical positions propounded by the early and by the later Yogācāra doctors. For example, Yoshifumi Ueda's work[76] has pointed out several areas of major differences in the interpretation of key concepts as expounded by Vasubandhu and Sthiramati on the one hand and by Dharmapāla on the other. Ueda's treatment clearly shows that Dharmapāla gave an idealistic cast to many terms which were not used in this way by Vasubandhu and Sthiramati. This idealistic tendency carried over into the works translated by Hsüan-tsang. However, many scholars have relied rather heavily for their knowledge of the Yogācāra upon Dharmapāla's accounts of the tradition, together with his exegesis of Vasubandhu's two short treatises (the *Viṃśatikā* and *Triṃśikā*), allowing this later idealistic thread of the school to speak for the whole of Yogācāra thought.[77] The problems resulting from not carefully delineating the two historically and philosophically different threads of the Yogācāra are obvious. Not distinguishing them, we are not only at a loss to determine which transmission is most faithful to the system's original form and content; we are equally incapable of being able to assert with any degree of accuracy what the actual positions originally were.

Hence, there is a pressing need for more translations of works by the earliest expounders of the school. Moreover, much work needs to be done in "a strictly *historico-philological* method,"[78] since our problems—particularly with respect to the Yogācāra—are greatly complicated by the fact that important terminology most often associated with the school has been misinterpreted and consequently mistranslated, not only by proponents of the later thread of the tradition but by modern-day Buddhologists as well. Terms such as *ālaya-vijñāna, cittamātra, vijñāna,* and *vijñaptimātra* that figure prominently in many Yogācāra texts have been woefully misinterpreted. They represent the central concepts in such works as the *Saṃdhinirmocana* and *Laṅkāvatāra* sūtras. And they are found in some of the writings of Asaṅga, most notably in his *Mahāyānasaṃgraha.* Though such terms are altogether absent from the *Tattva* chapter, because of their signal importance to the Yogācāra overall, it is necessary and useful, I feel, to pay some attention to them here, if only briefly.

As previously mentioned, one of Asaṅga's expedient devices *(upāya)* was the explication of an "ontological-psychological" model for detailing the evolution of consciousness that creates the seeming reality of the subject-object duality. Central to this model was the notion of the *ālayavijñāna* ("store-consciousness" or "underlying awareness"). According to this model, consciousness *(vijñāna),* impelled by *karma* (here, *former* deeds), hypostatizes the appearance of duality—though no such dualism exists in truth. The model asserts that consciousness occurs by evolving in eight forms: the first six are the five sense perceptions together with the mental perception; the seventh is the "defiled mind," or the consciousness deluded by the notion of a "self"; and an eighth consciousness is termed the *ālayavijñāna.* While the first mentioned five "evolutes" appear to be concerned with objective data and the sixth and seventh with subjective data, all seven consciousnesses function solely to reflect data supplied by the underlying store-consciousness, the *ālaya.*[79]

This model has led many Buddhologists to conclude that the Yogācāra considered the *ālayavijñāna* the ultimate reality. For example, E. J. Thomas in his *History of Buddhist Thought* states: "There is an ultimate reality, real beyond anything that can be asserted of what comes within the range of experience. This is thought *(citta)* or mind, not mind as existing in the variety in which it is experienced, but without any differentiation, and called store-consciousness *(ālayavijñāna).*"[80] However, to suppose that Asaṅga intended the *ālayavijñāna* as a synonym for ultimate reality is to disregard his own (as well as Vasubandhu's and Sthiramati's) statements to the contrary.

For Asaṅga, the *ālayavijñāna* concept is part of an innovative explanation of the old Buddhist doctrine of *nairātmya* ("non-self"). According to Mahāyāna thought, there is neither "self in the self" *(pudgala-* or *ātma-nairātmya),* nor "self in the dharmas" *(dharma-nairātmya);* but ordinary beings have the false notion that both these, i.e., subject and objects, exist in their own right. The *ālayavijñāna* theory is developed and expounded by Asaṅga in reply to the question, "How and why does this false notion arise?" It was not advanced by him as a metaphysical proposition.

Other of Asaṅga's writings also evidence that the *ālaya* is not proposed in an absolute sense. For example, in his *Abhidharmasamuccaya,* while addressing himself to the definition of the "aggregate of consciousness" *(vijñāna-skandha),* Asaṅga states: "What is the definition of the aggregate of consciousness? It is mind *(citta),* mental organ *(manas)* and also consciousness *(vijñāna).* And there, what is mind *(citta)*? It is the *ālayavijñāna. . . .*"[81]

So *citta* is equated with *ālayavijñāna,*[82] and both are included in the *vijñāna-skandha* (the aggregate of consciousness). But all five *skandhas* are *anitya* (impermanent), *duḥkha* (suffering), and *anātma* (without self), as Asaṅga himself notes later in that same text.[83]

There is perhaps no term more misunderstood and misinterpreted in the whole of Yogācāra scholarship than *cittamātra.* Viewed as at once marking the most characteristic feature of the school's philosophical doctrine and as, in fact, naming its ontological absolute, this term has come to represent for most scholars the very hallmark of the school. Its literal translation as "mind-only" is misleading, implying as it does an absolute idealism. Such a translation is especially mistaken with reference to Asaṅga's works, since for him the term lacks this absolutist connotation. *Cittamātra,* throughout the early Yogācāra, should more properly be rendered as "just thought" or "merely thought" and seen more appropriately as functioning within the realm of discourse concerned primarily with the meditative experience—that is, within discourse about spiritual *practice* as opposed to strictly philosophical theory. (The reader will remember that the earliest name of the school, *Yogācāra,* was intended to emphasize the primary importance of meditative technique as the means of gaining an unimpeded view of ultimate reality.)

Cittamātra is undoubtedly one of the most complex and difficult terms to get a handle on, for a number of reasons. It is an important term in Mahāyāna Buddhism as a whole and so occurs in both Yogācāra and Mādhyamika works. It occurs with *differing* meanings in various of the Mahāyāna sūtras which are said to serve as specific scriptural authorities for the Yogācāra school. It is used in different contexts, and with different intent, in what I have called the "early" and "later" Yogācāra. And finally, even within the "early" Yogācāra, i.e., within the works of Asaṅga and Vasubandhu, *cittamātra* (and its companion term *vijñaptimātra)* seems to have had at least three distinct, intentional uses, depending upon whether those doctors were addressing themselves to (1) technical information concerning the meditative experience per se, that is, to specific meditative contexts and practice; (2) common sense, prescriptive advice for ordinary beings overly attached to materiality (where it may be said to have had a "provisional meaning," marking a sort of intermediate stage in terms of general practice); or (3) the philosophical analysis and description of the cause of ordinary beings' suffering. It is here that we find the Yogācāra's important *epistemological* point that in every ordinary cognition, what is cognized is not an accurate portrayal of an object existing outside the mind but merely an object-like mental image *(vijñaptimātra)* of that; only a "conceptualized" object, one that is solely the product of constructive imagination.

It is impossible to go into detail on all the above points, especially in the space of an "Introduction." However, because of the overriding importance of the term *cittamātra,* an attempt must be made to look at its usages at least within the contexts of some early Mahāyāna sūtras and the commentarial works of the early Yogācāra. In so doing, we must remain constantly mindful of the changing contexts for the term, i.e., whether it is found in contexts related more to purely philosophical and theoretical speculation or in those associated primarily with spiritual and meditative practice.

Such a discussion should properly make mention of at least the following Mahāyāna sūtras; the *Daśabhūmikasūtra,* the *Bhadrapālasūtra,* the *Saṃdhinirmocanasūtra,* and the *Laṅkāvatārasūtra.* The *Daśabhūmikasūtra* [84] is not, strictly speaking, a sūtra of the Yogācāra class of literature, but it exercised influence on the Yogācāra, especially in its later developments. In the sixth chapter of this sūtra is found a well-known passage that goes: *cittamātram idaṃ yad idaṃ traidhātukam* ("These three realms [85] [the realms of desire, corporeal matter, and immateriality] are nothing but mind.") This passage has been commented upon by numerous Buddhist doctors of the Mahāyāna, both Mādhyamika [86] and Yogācarā, throughout its history. The context of the passage at first glance seems mainly to be philosophical. In fact, the quotation is centered within a discussion of the

Buddhist theory of "dependent origination" *(pratītyasamutpāda)*. The standard Mādhyamika interpretation of the passage is that the phrase does not deny external entities, but emphasizes that mere mind (or thought) conventionally *(saṃvṛtitas)* creates the external entities.[87] On the other hand, it is commonly held—by Mādhyamika theorists as well as many modern-day scholars—that for the Yogācāra it means the denial of all external entities. Of course, on the face of it, an idealistic interpretation of this passage does not seem particularly strange. However, one has reason to question it when one notes the other phrases immediately surrounding this one. Since all the other sentences, following and preceding, presuppose the traditional realistic ontology, this phrase seems unusual and rather isolated, to say the least. That fact led L. Schmithausen to conclude that the *Daśabhūmika* was probably not the place where the phrase was first formulated.[88] Some results of his important investigations are worth quoting in full:

> In fact, the sentence occurs also in at least one other old Mahāyānasūtra, namely the Pratyutpannabuddhasaṃmukha-avasthitasamādhisūtra, also called Bhadrapālasūtra, which was translated into Chinese by Lokakṣema as early as 179 A.D., i.e. more than one hundred years before the Daśabhūmikasūtra.
>
> As the longer title of this Sūtra shows, its main subject is a special kind of visionary meditation in which the Yogin sees himself face to face with any Buddha of the present time, especially with Amitābha or Amitāyus, the Buddha who resides in the western paradise Sukhāvatī. In the third chapter of this Sūtra, these apparitions of the Buddha visualized in meditation are compared with dream visions, with reflected images, and with the decaying corpses and skeletons visualized in the 'contemplation of the impure' *(aśubhabhāvanā)*. Just as these imaginary appearances, the Buddhas visualized in meditative concentration are also not really met by the meditating Bodhisattva but only projections of the Bodhisattva's

mind; and what the Bodhisattva should realize is precisely this fact that the visualized Buddha is nothing but mind *(cittam eva)*.

This ideality of the meditation-images, however, has to be extended to *all* phenomena: Just as a man, awaking from a dream, comprehends that all phenomena are illusory like dream visions, in the same way the reflection of the Bodhisattva who understands that in his meditation he did not really meet the Buddha culminates in the intuition of the universal ideality: "This whole world consisting of the three spheres is nothing but mind (cittamātram idaṃ [yad idaṃ?] traidhātukam). And why? Because [I see in the case of meditation that] it appears just as I imagine."[89]

Clearly, then, in this work which predates the *Daśabhūmikasūtra* (as well as the works of Asaṅga), the term *cittamātra* was first used within the context of the meditative practice.[90]

What is "just mind" or "wholly mind"? The earliest answer seems to have been: "The image *(ālambana; pratibimba)*[91] cognized during intense contemplation *(samādhi)*." It was an answer which intended to describe the "ideal" character of the *samādhi*-image, the object mentally visualized by the meditating yogin.

This seems to be true also of the initial instances of *cittamātra* (and of *vijñaptimātra)* in the *Saṃdhinirmocanasūtra*. It is especially noticeable in the eighth chapter of that work. There "the question is raised whether the images which are the object of meditation *(samādhigocarapratibimba)* are different from the mind *(citta)* or not. The answer is that they are *not* different from the mind because they are nothing but cognition *(vijñaptimātra)*."[92] While in the whole of Asaṅga's voluminous *Yogācārabhūmi* there is extremely sparse use of either *cittamātra* or *vijñaptimātra*[93] (the lengthy text, except for the *Bodhisattvabhūmi* section, obviously presupposing the realistic ontology of the Hīnayāna schools), yet in his *Mahāyānasaṃgraha* (chapter II) he quotes this passage from the *Saṃdhinirmocanasūtra:*

Maitreya asked: Lord, are those images cognized in meditation different from that mind (which cognizes them) or are they not different? The Lord answered: Maitreya, they are not different. And why? Because those images are nothing but conceptualization *(vijñaptimātra)*. Maitreya, I have explained that the meditative object *(ālambana)* of consciousness *(vijñāna)* is comprised of *(prabhāvita)* nothing but conceptualization *(vijñaptimātra)*.[94]

It is significant that this quotation, focusing as it does on the nature of the *meditative image,* is found in Asaṅga's *Mahāyānasaṃgraha* immediately following another quotation there, namely, the famous phrase from the *Daśabhūmikasūtra* alluded to earlier. Clearly, for Asaṅga the terms *cittamātra* and *vijñaptimātra* function preeminently within discourses pertaining to actual meditative instruction and practice.

The Yogācāra is indeed concerned first and foremost with the mind *(citta)*—its nature, development, and workings—precisely because it considers the mind so essential to the meditative processes. Thereby it is simultaneously the source of ultimate liberation. This is because meditation *(samādhi)* is not different from wisdom *(prajñā)*.[95] Awareness of the functioning of the mind is the meditative practice *par excellence,* since the realization that the meditative object visualized by the mind is created *by* the mind and is *nothing but* mind *(cittam eva* or *cittamātra)* is simultaneously the direct realization of *śūnyatā* itself, that is, of the voidness of both object and subject. There appears to be an object "out there," but this is realized in meditation to be nothing but the mind, or awareness. Moreover, through meditation, the subject itself is likewise seen to be illusory. There being a relative and mutual relationship between these two, neither object nor subject exists independently in its own right. This fact is realized directly in the meditative experience of the advanced yogin-bodhisattva. Speaking of the general progression of that meditative experience, Alex Wayman[96] has stated:

In yoga training, one should transfer the object to the mind, then eliminate all mental straying from the meditative object and avoid any alteration of the meditative object itself. In the final stage of such meditation, the object ceases to be the object, since the subject-object relation has been transcended. With the "eye of *prajñā*"—which is no "eye"—the meditator sees the entity in the form of the void: he has carried it back to the realm where it abides in itself, devoid of all adventitious relations, and so it is not the "object" of a "subject."

And again, important texts of the early Yogācāra make this process explicit. For example, in Rahula's words,[97] the *Mahāyānasūtrālaṅkāra* (chapter VI, verse 8 and commentary), states that:

the Bodhisattva, having realized that there is nothing more than thought *(citta)*, comes to the realization that that thought *(citta)* or "only thought" *(cittamātra)* itself does not exist, and thus realizing that there is no object *(grāhya)* or subject *(grāhaka)*, he is established in the Dharmadhātu.

Perhaps nothing offers better proof that the "declaration" of *cittamātra* is but an expedient device than the *Bhadrapālasūtra*. Schmithausen writes:[98]

we must not lose sight of the fact that the Bhadrapālasūtra merely intends to introduce into [the discussion] the unreality of phenomena and not to establish the mind as a higher reality. This is clear from the concluding verses where the Sūtra, after having enunciated its thesis that the Buddha visualized in meditation is nothing but mind and perceived only by the mind (i.e. that in this case mind perceives nothing but itself). "[But] the mind cannot cognize the mind, the mind cannot perceive the mind." . . . Thus, even the notion of mind (as something real) is only ignorance and has to be abandoned. The reduction of objects to the mind is thus merely a preliminary step towards the intuition of complete Emptiness.

It should be noted that this last statement by Schmithausen succinctly summarizes the essential process and goal of tantric meditation, and explains the preeminence accorded the Yogācāra school in the development of Buddhist tantra in general.[99]

The *Laṅkāvatārasūtra* is often singled out as a Mahāyāna sūtra associated with the Yogācāra, which straightforwardly propounds universal absolute idealism. It is certainly the case that one finds in the *Laṅkāvatārasūtra* abundant instances of the term *cittamātra,* all of which may be validly said *at least on the surface* to suggest full-blown idealism. Discussions are not found there of the *samādhi* image nor of other features of the meditative experience per se. Rather, the sūtra seems to speak directly of the ordinary person's situation. It says that all the *ordinary* objects one commonly assumes to exist as external realities are "nothing but mind."

For example, this sūtra at chapter III, verse 33, claims to quote the Buddha as saying:

> The external world is not, and the multiplicity of objects is what is seen of mind. Body, sense experience, dwelling place—I call just mind *(cittamātra).* [100]

Hence, it would seem that the sūtra makes a much more categorical statement of absolute idealism than any of the other works commonly associated with the Yogācāra—certainly more so than any of the Mahāyāna sūtras most often cited in this connection. Two brief comments must suffice initially in this regard. Firstly, the *Laṅkāvatāra* is itself not a sūtra which would be consonant with either Asaṅga's or Vasubandhu's early expositions of the Yogācāra. Second, even within the context of the *Laṅkāvatāra* the term *cittamātra* can be viewed as having an "intentional" usage, operating in a provisional-meaning *(neyārtha)* [101] sense only.

The *Laṅkāvatāra* is known to be a syncretic text, "more chaotic in composition, almost certainly because it grew gradually, collecting discussions on a great variety of topics which interested the idealistic movement." [102] Dr. Suzuki has described the scripture as "a memorandum kept by a Mahāyāna master, in which he put down perhaps all the teachings of importance accepted by the Mahāyāna followers of his day." [103] Given this general character of the work, a detailed explication of it clearly cannot be attempted here. But we should note, in passing, that the *Laṅkāvatāra* in chapter VI identifies the *ālayavijñāna* with a concept called the *Tathāgatagarbha* ("the womb of the 'Thus-gone one' "); and that such an identification is not accepted by the early Yogācāra of Asaṅga/Vasubandhu.[104]

As mentioned before, it is possible to view most of the "idealistic" proclamations of the sūtra as put forward only in a provisional sense, intended to divert sentient beings from their preoccupation with materialism.[105] In fact, this was the opinion of the great Tsoṅ-kha-pa, who referred to the *Laṅkāvatāra* as a sūtra of "provisional" or "indirect" meaning *(neyārtha)* requiring further interpretation (as opposed to one of "final" or "definitive" meaning, *nītārtha).* To bear out his assessment of the *Laṅkāvatāra,* Tsoṅ-kha-pa cites a verse drawn from that text: [106]

> In the way that a physician offers a medicine to one patient and a medicine to another patient, in that way the Buddhas teach mind-only for the sentient beings.

INTRODUCTION

As previously noted, the term *vijñaptimātra* is often used as a synonym for *cittamātra,* especially within meditative contexts, viz. chapter VIII of the *Saṃdhinirmocanasūtra.* Therefore, what has been said for the term *cittamātra* in such contexts holds equally for *vijñaptimātra.* We may here, however, allude to one other "intentional" usage of *vijñaptimātra.* While Asaṅga's *Mahāyānasaṃgraha* had treated of ten specific topics, it was Vasubandhu (in his commentary on the *Mahāyānasaṃgraha* and other early Yogācāra texts) who designated *vijñaptimātra* as the central conception of the school. Vasubandhu was first and foremost concerned with *philosophical* discourse. The shift in emphasis from discourse centering on *cittamātra* in a meditative context to that centering on *vijñaptimātra* in a philosophical context it seems was accomplished by Vasubandhu and prompted by his own unique genius as a popularizer of the tradition. In both of his famed short treatises, the *Viṃśatikā* and *Triṃśikā,* Vasubandhu stresses *vijñaptimātra,* "just representation" or "just conceptualization." It is generally held—as summarized, for example, by Kalupahana[107]—that:

> The *Viṃśatikā* is devoted to a refutation of the Realist's position and a philosophical justification of the Idealist's standpoint. It is mainly a polemical work. The *Triṃśikā* is devoted to a systematic treatment of the basic teachings of the Idealists.

An alternative and more accurate way of assessing the two treatises, I believe, is to see them as offering, in the first mentioned text, an analysis and description of the *cause* of ordinary beings' suffering, and in the second, an analysis and description of the *solution* to this problem.[108] Again, the *Viṃśatikā* illuminates the ordinary being's chief delusion, namely, his mistaking the commonly perceived universe of appearance to exist *as perceived* rather than as a universe distorted by conceptualization of all sorts. Indeed, this overlay of constructive imaginations *(kalpanā, vijñapti, vikalpa)* is all that we commonly contact and cognize. We do not see the thing as it really is; we see only a conceptualized thing. And this is precisely Vasubandhu's point (as it had been Asaṅga's also). All that we commonly perceive is *vijñaptimātra.* It is only "representation" or "just conceptualization." And because of this, it is not ultimate reality.

Addressing himself in the *Triṃśikā* to the solution of the problem of beings' suffering, Vasubandhu first succinctly lays out the model of the evolution of consciousness, detailing the eight consciousnesses as described here earlier, then describes the correct mode of cognizing ultimate reality. For example, the text begins:[109]

Because our ideation gives rise to the
False ideas of the ego and dharmas,
There are various revulsions of appearances.

Verse xx states:

Because of false discriminations,
Various things are falsely discriminated.
What is grasped by such false discrimination
Has no self-nature whatsoever.

The concluding sections read:

xxv. The supreme truth of all dharmas
Is nothing other than the True Norm (suchness).
It is forever true to its nature,
Which is the true nature of mind-only.
xxvi. Inasmuch as consciousness in its unawakened state
Is not in the abode of the reality of mind-only,

The six sense-organs, their objects, and the seeds of evil desires
Cannot be controlled and extirpated.

xxvii. To hold something before oneself,
And to say that it is the reality of mind-only,
Is not the state of mind-only,
Because it is the result of grasping.

xxviii. But when (the objective world which is) the basis of conditioning as well as the wisdom (which does the conditioning)
Are both eliminated,
The state of mind-only is realized,
Since the six sense-organs and their objects are no longer present.

xxix. Without any grasping and beyond thought
Is the supra-mundane wisdom (of bodhisattvahood)
Because of the abandonment of the habit-energy of various karmas and the six sense-organs as well as their objects,
The revulsion from relative knowledge to perfect wisdom is attained.

xxx. This is the realm of passionlessness or purity,
Which is beyond description, is good, and is eternal,
Where one is in the state of emancipation, peace, and joy.
This is the law of the Great Buddha.

Vijñapti ("conceptualization") and *vikalpa,* translated herein as "discursive thought," are synonyms in the works of both Asaṅga and Vasubandhu. Hence, for both, the ultimate insight *(prajñā)* is characterized as *nirvikalpa jñāna,* i.e., as knowledge that is completely freed of discursive thought, wholly apart from imaginative constructions or superimpositions. The often misinterpreted term, *vijñaptimātra,* therefore, which Vasubandhu made the hallmark of Yogācāra thought, refers not to a claim of absolute idealism but rather to that state of knowledge which arises when one directly realizes the *cause* of delusion, which is the realization that ordinarily all that we perceive is overlaid with and is solely *(mātra)* constructed images *(vijñapti)*. With such realization there is the concomitant arising of *prajñā* and the dissolution of both subject and object, seer and seen.

While treatises of the "later" thread of the Yogācāra employ the terms *vijñaptimātra* and *cittamātra* in senses that seemingly deny the existence of external objects altogether, such usage seems clearly to have arisen at a later historical and philological period.[110]

At any rate, all this terminology most often associated with treatments of the Yogācāra is conspicuously absent from Asaṅga's *Tattvārtha* chapter. Instead, the chapter presents a kind of nominalistic philosophy wherein the key terms are *vastu* and *prajñapti* ("given thing" or "basis of the name" and "designation," respectively). These terms will be taken up in the next section.

Contents of the Chapter

The *Tattva* chapter addresses itself directly to the problem of correctly assessing and verifying knowledge of reality as it really is *(yathābhūtam)*. The chapter's opening phrase, *tattvārtha katamaḥ,* "What is knowledge of reality?", prefaces a thoroughgoing analysis of this problem according to Mahāyāna thought.

The compound term *tattvārtha* requires some explication here. It is composed of two Sanskrit words, each of which has numerous connotations. A literal rendering of *tattva* is "thatness" (*tat* = "that" and *tva* = "ness"), or "thusness," and refers to the true or actual state of things or affairs, i.e., their reality in themselves, apart from all adventitious elements or subjective biases. Etymologically, the term shares affinity with *tathatā,* which is generally translated "suchness" and which often appears as a synonym for *śūnyatā* (voidness), the true state of things, according to the Mahāyāna.

Though Asaṅga's work employs the term *tathatā* in a way consistent with Mahāyāna usage, it is employed sparingly, and clear preference is given to *tattva* as the key term of the chapter. As a technical term, it is interesting that *tattva* is often used to delineate distinct and individual realities, especially in treatises associated with yoga schools.[111] In this translation the term is consistently rendered by "reality."

Artha, which I translate as "knowledge" or "knowing," is a complex word in Sanskrit, having many connotations and covering a whole range of referents. It may be rendered by "aim," "goal," "purpose," "thing," "object," "meaning," "nature," and other translations, though some are more typically used in certain contexts than others. Though "knowing" and "knowledge" are unusual translations for *artha,* these renderings seem, in fact, the most appropriate in the context of the chapter, since Asaṅga's chief theme throughout it is the delineation of the various types of knowledge about reality. In the earliest sections of the chapter *artha* is shown several times to be a synonym for *jñāna* (i.e. "knowledge" or "cognitive activity"). Hence—as I hope a reading of the entire chapter will verify for the reader—"knowing" in the title and "knowledge" in the translation proper are translations dictated by the general thrust of the work.

One might expect that "meaning" would be the more normal rendering here, but this term could prove inappropriate and even confusing in the context of the chapter. While the chapter's exegesis, the *Tattvārthaviniścaya,* uses *artha* in the sense of "object" or "concrete referent" of a name, it does so only with reference to ordinary beings' *inferior* understanding. The use of the term "meaning" almost invariably leads to involvement with ideas like the Augustinian conception of language and the so-called "correspondence theory of meaning" wherein "meaning is correlated with the word. It is the object for which the word stands."[112] We usually think of "meaning" in such a correspondence theory of language as referring solely to the "object of knowledge." But within the context of Asaṅga's epistemology, "meaning" would necessarily have to have a dual sense, encompassing both the object of knowledge and knowledge itself. The "meaning" of reality must refer to the object (here, reality) *as known,* i.e., to reality both as an object and as a direct knowledge-experience wherein object and subject dissolve in a "not-two" realization.

There is another reason why "meaning" was judged inappropriate in the context of the chapter. The term "meaning" generally appears in contexts where some adjective or substantive (here, "reality") is being defined, clarified, illuminated, etc. But, as Wittgenstein rightly noted, a substantive makes us look for a thing—an object or quality—that corresponds to it. Now, not only Wittgenstein, but Asaṅga as well, was at pains to show that this "essentialism" offshoot of the "correspondence theory of meaning" was misleading and not conducive to an understanding of reality as it really is. In the *Tattva* chapter as well as in his exegesis, Asaṅga argues against this mode of thinking. He says that ordinary beings (who possess the most "inferior" knowledge of reality) believe that a name stands for a thing and that each thing has a name. Moreover, because of this assumption, ordinary beings believe that names (which have arisen purely through convention and not through insight into the true state of things) accurately characterize the nature (or essence) of the things to which they are applied. Asaṅga argues strenuously, as do all the proponents of *śūnyatā* (i.e., voidness of essence), against this theory of essentialism.

In summary, *tattva,* in Asaṅga's usage, refers to the various *realities, as known* (i.e., experienced) by diverse beings; and the compound term, *tattvārtha,* denotes the various *kinds of knowledge* about reality. *Artha* is rendered herein as "knowledge" or "knowing" for the sake of consistency as well as to highlight the main thrust of the chapter.

Though not a lengthy text, the chapter addresses quite a number of topics, each of which may be seen as lending direct support to the central theme, the explication of how the bodhisattva should view reality. The chapter divides itself into four sections.

I. First is a detailed delineation of the goal—i.e., true

knowledge of ultimate reality—and of the preparatory practices for the bodhisattva seeking it. This section runs from the initial paragraph up through the declaration of the "way of nonproliferation."

II. Immediately following there is a brief but succinct section of passages in more or less debate style in which Asaṅga addresses the "philosophical reasoning" that proves the inexpressible character of all dharmas. This section runs up to the description of "voidness rightly conceptualized."

III. Next there follows an even briefer discussion that provides scriptural authority for this proper view and understanding of "suchness" as outlined above. This section mentions and explicates quotations from the *Bhavasaṃkrānti-sūtra,* the *Arthavargīya,* and the *Saṃtha-Kātyāyana-sūtra.* It runs up to the final declaration of the authority of the scriptures and of the "Tathāgata's lineage of trustworthy persons."

IV. The final division of the chapter is equal in length to the first section. Here Asaṅga discusses the faults of "discursive," undisciplined thought *(vikalpa)* and the means of coming to thoroughly comprehend its workings. Because discursive thought and conceptualization of all kinds cloud our view of ultimate reality, Asaṅga here takes pains to delineate and analyze such thought. The discussion points out that the whole process of distortion "is composed of two elements only: discursive thought, and the given thing which becomes the mental support of discursive thought" and that "these two are mutually produced *(anyonya hetuka).*" Indeed, this is one of the crowning statements of the chapter, for—in much the same way that Vasubandhu would later declare *vijñapti-mātra* ("conceptualization only") to be the chief problem in ordinary beings' perception of reality—Asaṅga here likewise defines discursive thought as the chief culprit,[113] that which robs beings of a true view of reality. Eight kinds of *vikalpa* are enumerated. Then follows a discussion of the means and equipment to which a bodhisattva should resort in order to completely comprehend and thereby combat such thought. In general, the method prescribed is to view such thought merely as thought, particular designations as "just designations" *(prajñapti-mātra)*. The accomplished bodhisattva should recognize, the chapter states, that "there is just the mere semblance of essential nature through designations" and he/she[114] should see designations claiming to distinguish particularity "with a not-two meaning." Such a view is attained with the attainment of nonattachment and nonclinging. The ultimate goal described by the chapter for the bodhisattva is the attainment of the "complete cessation of discursive thought along with the [perceived] given thing." This state is defined as the "Parinirvāṇa of the Great Vehicle." The chapter closes with a description of the benefits and the concomitant duties attained by the bodhisattva thus matured.

It may be helpful at this point to summarize the specific topics addressed by the chapter in a bit more detail (the Sanskrit terms are explained in the commentary proper). The text begins with the pronouncement by Asaṅga that knowledge of reality may be viewed as being of two sorts: (1) knowledge of all the dharmas as they are in themselves *(bhūtatā)* and (2) knowledge of all the dharmas as they exist phenomenally, in totality *(sarvatā)*. These are the two kinds of knowledge possessed by the Tathāgatas.[115] In fact, both amount to the same knowledge since, we are told later, that knowledge is the knowledge of the inexpressible essential nature of all dharmas, void in essence, and which whether viewed noumenally or phenomenally is the same *(sama)*.

Immediately following this twofold delineation, an alternate fourfold analysis is given. We are told that there are four kinds of *tattvārtha,* i.e.: (1) the so-called knowledge possessed by ordinary beings and based on a common consensus of language; (2) that kind claimed and posited by logicians; (3) that kind of knowledge possessed by the Hīnayāna practitioners; and (4) that knowledge possessed by the Buddhas and bodhisattvas, which is the supreme and proper mode of knowledge. In other words, Asaṅga begins the chapter by defining the superior knowledge of reality. He then retraces, through the fourfold analysis, the various types of knowledge of reality, ending again with this superior knowledge. The elucidation of this last type of *tattvārtha* is the major concern of the chapter.

There follows a brief description of each of the four *tattvārthas.* In discussing the last two of these, i.e., those two which belong to the two classes of Buddhist practitioners, Asaṅga also delineates the respective meditative methodology that gives rise to each mode of knowledge. For example, he tells us that the śrāvakas and pratyekabuddhas (of the Hīnayāna) attain to a clearer knowledge of reality than do ordinary beings or logicians because they have attained the destruction of the "outflows" *(āsravas)* of hatred, greed, and delusion. Having done so, their knowledge is completely purified of, and hence unhindered by, the defilement *(kleśa)* "obscurations" or obstructions. Moreover, Asaṅga states, their clear vision with respect to reality has arisen because they have penetrated the meaning of the Four Noble Truths and, concomitant with that, have comprehended *pudgala-nairātmya* (the selflessness or nonsubstantiality of the "person" or "self").

How does the superior knowledge of reality possessed by the Buddhas arise? This the bodhisattva earnestly seeks to realize. Asaṅga answers: The knowledge of the Buddhas is completely purified of the "obscurations to the knowable" *(jñeyāvaraṇa)* i.e., the last vestiges of subjective biases which block or obscure the true view of reality as it is. Such knowledge is completely freed of all discursive thought. It is *nirvikalpa jñāna.* Their knowledge has attained such purity because they have comprehended *dharmanairātmya* (the selflessness of all dharmas) and, according to Asaṅga, because they have understood the inexpressible sameness *(samatā)* of essential nature for all dharmas. The chapter further defines this sameness as "the sameness of the essential nature of verbal designation and the nondiscursive knowable." Asaṅga's subsequent elucidation is based upon a detailed analysis of names (or designations) and knowables, the given things of experience.

Correct knowledge arises, then, for the bodhisattva who, having entered the "Path of Instruction,"[116] strives unceasingly to comprehend *śūnyatā,* the void nature of all dharmas. Having done so, he is said to know Suchness *(tathatā)* directly, i.e., reality as it really is *(yathābhūtam),* by viewing it in accordance with the Middle Path *(madhyamā pratipat)* mode of view.

Since this chapter is addressed specifically to bodhisattvas seeking such knowledge, Asaṅga then gives a brief description of the *practices* to which the bodhisattva should resort. The bodhisattva should not seek the Nirvāṇa of the Hīnayānists but, working for the welfare of beings in whatever saṃsāric existence he/she is in, should practice the six perfections *(pāramitās),* remain equable, and remain firmly rooted in the realization of śūnyatā.

Having described the practices which the bodhisattva seeking supreme knowledge of reality should take up, Asaṅga now focuses upon the *doctrinal* side of the chapter. He first explicates the philosophical views which are unacceptable for such a bodhisattva, and then addresses those views which are acceptable.

Asaṅga regards two philosophical positions as being unacceptable to the bodhisattva intent on gaining supreme knowledge of reality: (1) the position (of ordinary beings) which claims that there is a real correspondence existing between verbal designations *(prajñapti)* and dharmas, i.e., which asserts that names *(nāma)* accurately characterize the true nature of things; and (2) the *nihilist* position which wrongly conceptualizes voidness, either (a) by asserting that only designations exist, *not* the things designated (Asaṅga shows that in the absence of things, designations would not occur either); or (b) by claiming that "absolutely everything is nonexistent" (Asaṅga shows that the notion of voidness is dependent upon the existence, in some way, of the void or voided thing).

Asaṅga then presents, in debate style, a refutation of the ordinary being's position. His own exegesis on the chapter fills out this refutation by considering the assumed "real correspondence" between names and things from a number of different perspectives. Asaṅga's conclusion is that the bodhisattva should properly regard designations as just designations *(prajñaptimātra)*, as neither possessing nor engendering essential nature *(svabhāva)*. On the other hand, designations are not to be regarded as being completely devoid of essential nature since, in truth, they do possess the essential nature of śūnyatā, which is, for Asaṅga, an existent.

When he takes up his arguments against those nihilists who wrongly conceptualize voidness—whether their philosophical position upholds the real existence of designations [i.e., *prajñaptivādins*] or denies the real existence of both designations and their referents [*vaināśikas*], Asaṅga's remarks can clearly be viewed as intending to refute both the positions of some "insiders" (here, adherents of the Mādhyamika doctrine) and those of "outsiders" (non-Buddhists). These "insiders" are those Buddhists who have misunderstood and misinterpreted the doctrine of śūnyatā, wrongly understanding it as extreme nihilism. According to Asaṅga, the prajñaptivādin's position is completely untenable, for such a one wishes to assert that designations exist though their referents do not. But since he completely denies the possibility of referents for these designations, how would they come to be? Therefore, in effect, he denies *both* reality and designations. But such a position, we are told, is that of the "chief nihilist" *(pradhāna nāstika);* and a person claiming this position should be avoided by one treading the Buddhist path, since "he has strayed far away from our Dharma-Vinaya."

The position of those "insiders" and "outsiders" who have most gravely misconceptualized voidness is that "absolutely everything is nonexistent in truth." Such a universal denial would negate the very *possibility* of voidness itself. Thus, this position, we are shown by Asaṅga both here and in his exegesis of the chapter (wherein he takes up the explication of the three *svabhāvas),* is unacceptable to the bodhisattva seeking supreme knowledge of reality.

Now, the text takes up the discussion of rightly or properly conceptualized voidness, which it clearly equates with the philosophical views acceptable to the bodhisattva seeking supreme knowledge of reality. Under this heading Asaṅga brings in quotations from the Buddhist canonical scriptures. Those views which are acceptable to the bodhisattva are those described in the *Bhavasaṃkrānti-sūtra,* the Arthavargīya of the *Sutta-Nipāta* and the *Saṃtha-Kātyāyana-sūtra.*[117] These scriptures clearly explicate the true nature of all dharmas as being empty of self *(nairātmya)* and inexpressible *(nirabhilāpya)*. Such an understanding characterizes the true Mahāyāna view, the Middle Path *(madhyamā-pratipat)*. This philosophical position is the view which is acceptable to the bodhisattva seeking supreme knowledge of reality.

Having finished his description of the proper, Middle Path, view which the bodhisattva on the Path of Instruction should adopt, Asaṅga now warns the bodhisattva of the pitfalls of discursive thought *(vikalpa)*. He begins by saying that it is "precisely owing to lack of understanding of that Suchness" that eight kinds of discursive thought and the "three bases" arise for "immature beings" and because of these, the whole round of existence (i.e., *saṃsāra*) is produced and operates. Therefore, the bodhisattva intent on knowledge of reality as it is should carefully investigate and guard against these eight kinds of discursive thought. He should do so by means of the four "thorough investigations" *(paryeṣaṇas)* and the four kinds of "knowing precisely, in detail" *(yathābhūtaparijñānas)*. Asaṅga explains each of these in accordance with the Middle Path mode of viewing.

The chapter concludes with a brief description of the benefits *(anuśaṃsas)* and concomitant duties *(karaṇīyas)* which accrue for the bodhisattva who, having attained the cessation *(nirodha)* of discursive thoughts along with given things *(vastus)*—and, thereby, the cessation of all proliferation *(prapañca)*—stands firmly fixed in the realization of "the most splendid knowledge of reality."

Notes to the Introduction

1. There are other texts bearing this same title. For example, M. Demiéville has published work on a text entitled the *Yogācārabhūmi* which was authored by a Saṅgharakṣa (see *Bulletin de l'école française d'éxtrême Orient* 44 [1954]). In this same work by Demiéville there are two other texts mentioned bearing the name *Yogācārabhūmi:* one being composed by Buddhasena and being a wholly Hīnayāna treatise, and the other bearing simply the title "Yogācārabhūmi of the Bodhisattva." This latter text, according to Demiéville, is "a small yoga manual of the Mahāyāna translated into Chinese circa 300." See Wayman, *Analysis of the Śrāvakabhūmi Manuscript,* p. 41.

2. The five major divisions and their contents as summarized in Bu-ston's *History of Buddhism,* pp. 55–56 are as follows: (1) The *Bahubhūmikavastu,* or *Bhūmivastu,* which expounds the Yogācāra doctrine according to seventeen subjects and hence is comprised of seventeen volumes. (2) *Viniścaya saṃgrahaṇī,* a commentary on the *Bahubhūmikavastu.* (3) *Vastu saṃgrahaṇī,* which "demonstrates the order in which [the contents of the *Bahubhūmikavastu*] should be combined in accordance with the three codes of Scripture." (4) *Paryāya saṃgrahaṇī,* giving the synonyms of words expressing the different subjects"; and (5) The *Vivaraṇa saṃgrahaṇī,* which "enlarges upon the methods of teaching [adopted by the preceding works]."

3. The seventeen "bhūmis" of the *Bahubhūmikavastu* are the following:

1. *Pañcavijñānakāyasaṃprayukta bhūmi*
2. *Manobhūmi*
3. *Savitarkāsavicārā bhūmi*
4. *Avitarkā-vicāramātrā bhūmi*
5. *Avitarkā-avicārā bhūmi*

6. *Samāhitā bhūmi*
7. *Asamāhitā bhūmi*
8. *Sacittikā bhūmi*
9. *Acittikā bhūmi*
10. *Śrutamayī bhūmi*
11. *Cintāmayī bhūmi*
12. *Bhāvanāmayī bhumi*
13. *Śrāvakabhūmi*
14. *Pratyekabuddhabhūmi*
15. *Bodhisattvabhūmi*
16. *Sopādhikā bhūmi*
17. *Nirupādhikā bhūmi*

The Sanskrit titles of the *bhūmis* are provided in Bhattacharya's edition of the *Yogācārabhūmi,* p. 3. Only the *Bodhisattvabhūmi* (in the two editions used for the present work) was entirely preserved in the Sanskrit, the rest of the treatise being preserved only in the Chinese until the retranslating and editing work of Bhattacharya.

4. The great sage Paramārtha is noted as having imported into China the texts of Asaṅga and Vasubandhu. Takakusu in his *Essentials of Buddhist Philosophy,* p. 81, gives 548 A.D. as the date of Paramārtha's arrival in China. An earlier date has been suggested by Nariman in *Literary History of Sanskrit Buddhism,* p. 97, where he states: "Paramārtha imported from Magadha to China the works of Asaṅga and Vasubandhu in the year of 539" (A.D.). Even Nariman's date makes the arrival in China of other works by Asaṅga and Vasubandhu some 121 years after Asaṅga's *Bodhisattvabhūmi* appeared there.

5. See the Wayman and Wayman edition of the *Śrī-Mālā-sūtra,* p. 9.

6. The other five texts were the *Mahāyānasūtrālaṃkāra* (of Maitreya), the *Śikṣāsamuccaya* and the *Bodhicaryāvatāra* (of Śantideva), Āryaśura's *Jātakamāla,* and the *Udānavarga.*

7. *Bu-ston, History,* Part I, p. 49.

8. The *Viniścaya saṃgrahaṇī* is Asaṅga's own exegetical division accompanying his *Bahubhūmikavastu,* both being sections of his *Yogācārabhūmi.* The Tibetan text of the *Tattvārtha-viniścaya saṃgrahaṇī,* located in the *PTT,* is the one used in the present study. There is no extant Sanskrit text, though the work is available in the Chinese *(Taishō Tripiṭaka,* vol. XXX).

9. According to the Mahāyāna, a bodhisattva experiences ten stages. Both Tāranātha's (p. 160) and Bu-ston's (Part I, p. 140) *Histories* state that Asaṅga

attained the rank of a third-stage bodhisattva. A detailed description of the ten stages may be found in the *Daśabhūmika* and *Saṃdhinirmocana sūtras.*

10. These translations for *prabhākarī,* along with others, are given by Dayal in *Bodhisattva Doctrine,* p. 286.

11. This definition is given in the *Mahāyānasūtrālaṅkāra,* p. 182, cited by Dayal, *Bodhisattva Doctrine,* p. 286.

12. Dayal, *Bodhisattva Doctrine,* p. 286.

13. Ibid., p. 287. Summarizing the attainments of a third-stage bodhisattva, Dayal writes, "He experiences and acquires the four *dhyānas,* the four non-material *samāpattis,* the four *brahmavihāras* and the five *abhijñās.*" The four Sanskrit terms in this passage refer to specific attainments of meditative practice, as follows: the four *dhyānas* represent the four successive stages of meditative trance, or complete concentration, which are marked by (1) concentration accompanied by joy and reflection; (2) concentration accompanied by joy and the absence of reflection; (3) concentration that is equable and freed of joy; and (4) concentration that is supremely equable, freed of joy or pain. The nonmaterial *samāpattis* or "attainments" refer to the meditator's station wherein he abides in the sphere of the infinity (1) of space; (2) of perception, or consciousness; (3) of nothing-at-all; and (4) of neither ideation nor nonideation. (These *samāpattis* are referred to by Asaṅga in the Chapter on Knowing Reality under the discussion of the "Saṃtha," master practitioner of meditation.)

The four *brahmavihāras* or "sublime abodes" are also known as *apramāṇāni,* or "measureless meditations." The meditations consist of the cultivation of the feelings of (1) *maitrī,* love or friendliness; (2) *karuṇā,* compassion; (3) *muditā,* sympathetic joy; and (4) *upekṣā,* or supreme equanimity.

Lastly, the *abhijñās* refer to the attainments of the supernormal faculties including: (1) *divyaṃ cakṣuḥ,* or divine vision, which pertains to the ability of seeing the various passing aways and rebirths of beings; (2) *divyaṃ śrotraṃ,* divine hearing; (3) *parasya ceta paryāya-jñānam,* or knowing the makeup of others' thoughts; (4) *pūrva-nivāsānusmṛti-jñānam,* memory of former lives; and (5) *ṛddhi-vidhi-jñānam,* or mastery of magical powers.

14. The chief traditional accounts are those provided by Tāranātha and Bu-ston, which are available in translation (see the bibliography).

15. Paramārtha's account has been translated by Takakusu in "The Life of Vasu-bandhu by Paramārtha."

16. Alex Wayman, in his *Analysis of the Śrāvakabhūmi Manuscript,* p. 23, has suggested approximate dates for Asaṅga of c. 375–430 A.D. These are in sufficiently close agreement with Sylvain Lévi's conclusion in his edition of

the *Mahāyāna-sūtrālaṃkāra,* II, 1–2 Considering the biographical accounts given by Tāranātha and Bu-ston, as well as Asaṅga's remarkable accomplishments in terms of training, writing, and teaching, it might not be incorrect to add an additional ten years to both sides of this span, giving approximate dates of 365–440 A.D. Warder in *Indian Buddhism,* p. 436, suggests earlier dates for Asaṅga, giving 290–360 A.D., but he offers no supporting evidence for such dates.

17. Tāranātha, *History,* p. 154.

18. Ibid., p. 154.

19. Tāranātha's account, ibid., p. 155, gives the woman's name as Prakāśaśīlā.

20. Bu-ston, *History,* pp. 36–37 describes the three-fold destruction of the Dharma in India, which had preceded Asaṅga's birth.

21. According to Nariman's *Literary History of Sanskrit Buddhism,* p. 96, and Wayman, *Analysis,* p. 25, all the three brothers were initially given the name Vasubandhu, but only for the middle brother did the name remain throughout adult life.

22. Tāranātha's *History,* p. 155, tells us that Asaṅga was born "with auspicious marks." Bu-ston, *History,* p. 137, says that Prasannaśīlā "drew on [her sons'] tongues the letter *A* and performed all the other rites in order to secure for them an acute intellectual faculty."

23. Tāranātha, *History,* p. 156.

24. Cf., Wayman, *Analysis,* p. 25.

25. Ibid., pp. 25–30.

26. For further details on this sect, see Bareau's *Les Sectes bouddhiques du Petit Véhicule,* p. 182.

27. Cf., in Wayman, *Analysis,* p. 31: ". . . Asaṅga, after entering the Sarvāstivādin school, sought in vain to understand voidness *(śūnyatā)* and fell into profound despair. Then came the arhat Piṇḍola from eastern *(pūrva)* Videha, and with his instruction Asaṅga penetrated the 'small vehicle' *(hīnayāna).*"

28. There is enough internal evidence provided by the works written by Asaṅga himself to enable us to list some of the Mahāyāna scriptures which were influential to him. For example, in addition to the Prajñā literature, with which he was certainly familiar, the *Saṃdhinirmocana sūtra* figures prominently. It is clear from the *Tattvārtha* chapter that he had also studied the *Bhavasaṃkrānti sūtra* (a text which the *Mahāvyutpatti* (no. 1379) mentions as among the oldest Mahāyāna texts) as well as works such as the *Sutta nipāta,* the *Aṅguttara Nikāya* and the *Saṃtha Kātyāyana sūtra* of the Lesser

Vehicle. The *Mahāyānasūtrālaṅkāra* and the other works attributed to Maitreya were certainly known to him. It is possible, though not established with certainty, that he may also have been familiar with the *Laṅkāvatāra-sūtra* and with the *Mahāyānaśraddhotpāda,* as well. In fact, judging from quotations included in his own written treatises, one could say that Asaṅga was well versed in all the Āgamas as well as many of the early and important Mahāyāna scriptures and their commentaries.

29. Tāranātha, *History,* p. 156. Tāranātha's account continues: "the nature of the Tantra and the *maṇḍala* of the *abhiṣeka* are not clear, though the latter appears to have been the *māyājāla-maṇḍala,* because this ācārya [i.e., Asaṅga's guru at that time] practiced the *maitreya-sādhana* with the *māyājāla-tantra.*" Under these circumstances, Asaṅga began his propitiation of Maitreya Buddha.

30. Other names associated with the mountain retreat are *Gur-pa-parvata* and *Gurupāda.* See Tāranātha's *History,* p. 156.

31. Tāranātha, *History,* p. 157.

32. Ibid.

33. This spelling is given by Bu-ston in his *History,* p. 138. Tāranātha's spelling, *History,* p. 157, is "Acintya," meaning "inconceivable," or "surpassing thought." S. C. Dass in his *A Tibetan-English Dictionary,* p. 592, makes "Acinta" synonymous with "Ajānta," the famed South Indian Buddhist monastic institution.

34. It is interesting that Lord Maitreya is often depicted as "being full of light" or as "flooding all with great rays of light." Such a description becomes associated with Asaṅga also, both in regard to his attainment of the third bodhisattva stage, *prabhākarī,* as well as to his successful accomplishment of the "sunlight samādhi" *(sūryaprabhā-samādhi).* This latter accomplishment, according to Paramārtha's account, was the direct result of a practice taught to him by Lord Maitreya. The sunlight samādhi is said to enable its successful practitioner to thoroughly understand everything.

35. These two verses are quoted verbatim in both Tāranātha's (p. 157–58) and Bu-ston's (p. 138) histories.

36. This according to Bu-ston, *History,* p. 139. Tāranātha's *History,* p. 158, differs slightly. He says: "Only a woman wine-seller saw him carry a pup. As a result, she later became enormously rich. A poor porter saw only the toes. As a result, he reached the stage of *samādhi* and attained *sādhāraṇa-siddhi.*"

37. Bu-ston's *History,* p. 139.

38. According to Buddhist cosmology, the Tuṣita heaven rests some 160,000 *yojanas* above the Yama heaven and 320,000 *yojanas* above sea level.

In it reside all the heavenly illuminating deities who are said to shed light upon the world. This heaven figures prominently in Buddhist lore, being that realm to which Mahāmāyā, Gautama Buddha's mother, went after her death, and the station of all bodhisattvas just prior to their final incarnation on earth as Buddhas. Therefore, Lord Maitreya, the future Buddha, is said to reside in Tuṣita at present. For further details on Buddhist cosmology, see McGovern's *A Manual of Buddhist Philosophy.*

39. Bu-ston's *History,* p. 139, mentions "50 or 53 human years," though it notes: "The scholiast of the *Yogācārya-bhūmi* in his turn says that he resided there six months and heard (the Doctrine of Maitreya)." Tāranātha's *History,* p. 159, states, "According to some others, he spent fifteen human years in Tuṣita. Different views like these are current. However, according to the popular belief prevalent in India and Tibet, he spent fifty human years (in Tuṣita). This calculation of fifty years appears to be based on counting every half year as one year, for the Indians say that he actually spent twenty-five years there."

40. The "Five Books" attributed to Maitreya are: (1) the *Mahāyānasūtrālaṅkāra;* (2) *Madhyānta-Vibhaṅga;* (3) *Dharmadharmatā-vibhaṅga;* (4) *Abhisamayālaṅkāra;* and the (5) *Uttaratantra.* There are various editions and translations of some of these texts.

41. Tāranātha's *History,* p. 160, says that this vihāra was located in a forest called Veluvana, in Magadha. Here Asaṅga taught the Mahāyāna doctrine to eight chosen disciples, who all became famed for their mastery of the sūtras and later themselves preached the Mahāyāna. Hence, that vihāra became known as the abode "from which the Dharma again sprouted."

42. The problem of whether Asaṅga's teacher, Maitreya, was an actual historical person or simply Asaṅga's meditative, tutelary deity has long been an issue of concern to Buddhologists working with the Yogācāra. Anyone conversant with the details of Asaṅga's biography will be aware of the fact that his principal teacher was Maitreya, who is also referred to in some texts as Maitreyanātha. However, the chief debate has centered around whether Maitreya was an historical figure or the mythical figure of the same name who, according to Buddhist cosmology, represents the "Future Buddha."

All the traditional accounts—Bu-ston's, Tāranātha's and even Paramārtha's—assert that Asaṅga ascended to the Tuṣita heaven (i.e., that of the Future Buddha) and that there he received teachings from Maitreya. Many modern scholars, however, have attempted to prove that Maitreya was, in fact, a historical person who instructed Asaṅga in the flesh. Strong proponents of the historical theory are G. Tucci (see his *On Some Aspects of the Doctrines of Maitreya (nātha) and Asaṅga)*, H. Ui (in his "Maitreya as a Historical Personage"), and Hara-Prasad Shastri (in *Indian Historical Quarterly, 1* [1925], 465 f.).

Though the above scholars advanced sound arguments to prove their position, the debate took a different turn when M. Paul Demiéville, in his "La Yogācārabhūmi de Saṅgharakṣa" *Bulletin de l'école française d'extrême Orient*, 44, (1954), 381 and 386, reversed the argument, claiming that there was little reason to argue for a historical personage when valid texts amply attest to the contrary. Demiéville supported his claim by referring to the work of Sthiramati, a famed disciple of Asaṅga, wherein Sthiramati regards Maitreya as having been only Asaṅga's tutelary deity. Of course, the importance of the debate lies in the fact that a number of texts—the "Five Books"—are attributed to Maitreya, or Maitreyanātha. If it is accepted that Maitreya was a meditative or mythical figure, to whom do we attribute authorship of these works?

My own researches led me to make a comparative study of four *Tattva* chapters, in the course of which it became clear that the works attributed to Maitreya differed in key respects from the writings of Asaṅga. Sthiramati's account notwithstanding, it seems quite likely that these works were indeed written not by Asaṅga but by a historical personage named Maitreya who was associated with and taught Asaṅga. The fact that Asaṅga himself is referred to as "Maitreyanātha" is indicative only of his great respect for his teacher, Maitreya.

43. Bu-ston, *History*, p. 140, describes the *Abhidharmasamuccaya* as being "a summary (of the teaching that is) common to all the three Vehicles. . . . It is a Mahāyānistic treatise, but this does not contradict the fact that it demonstrates the subjects that refer to all the three Vehicles." It is further said to be an abridgment of the first two sections of the *Yogācārabhūmi*.

44. The text of Asaṅga's *Mahāyānasaṃgraha* is available in an excellent three-volume French edition edited and translated by Étienne Lamotte.

45. Asaṅga's works show clear evidence of his familiarity with the *Prajñā* literature. It is known that he wrote at least one commentary on the text of the *Vajracchedika-sūtra*, a metrical commentary called the *Vajracchedika-prajñāpāramitāsūtraśāstrakārikā*. This text is edited and translated in Giuseppe Tucci's *Minor Buddhist Texts, Part I*.

46. Tāranātha's *History*, p. 161.

47. Ibid., pp. 165–66.

48. Ibid., p. 166.

49. Ibid.

50. It is important to remember that according to the traditional accounts, Asaṅga had completed all his own written works before converting his half-brother Vasubandhu to the Mahāyāna and taking him as a student.

51. Bu-ston, *History,* p. 142, and Tāranātha, *History,* p. 167.

52. By the time of the great king Aśoka, c. 250 B.C., the two major factions of Buddhist followers, i.e., the Mahāsāṅghikas and the Sthāviras, had splintered and developed into eighteen distinct subsects. Vasubandhu is said to have mastered the details of each of these sects' scriptures and to have discerned—according to Tāranātha, *History,* p. 168—"where the Vinaya-s and Sūtra-s of the different schools differed. . . ." Such intellect and training well qualified him to write the famed *Abhidharmakośa.*

53. According to Bu-ston's *History,* p. 144, Asaṅga told Vasubandhu this about his previous births. Moreover, according to both Tāranātha and Bu-ston, Vasubandhu had prayed for a vision of Asaṅga's tutelary deity, Maitreya, but with no success. Asaṅga informed him that he would be unable to do so in his lifetime as Vasubandhu. Some accounts say this was because Vasubandhu had once deprecated the Mahāyāna, and others, that he had scoffed at Asaṅga and his work.

54. According to Tāranātha's account, *History,* p. 167. Bu-ston does not mention the place where the Ārya passed away. Rājagṛha is best known in Buddhist history as the site of the "First Council" held immediately following the Buddha's passing away.

55. In this regard the school is clearly the forerunner of later developments within the Mahāyāna such as the Ch'an school in China, so named because of its emphasis on meditation *(ch'an* = Skt. *dhyāna* and *samādhi).* The Yogācāra and the later Ch'an school also share the position that meditation *(samādhi)* and wisdom *(prajnā)* are not different. Rather, as the Ch'an text *The Platform Sūtra* states (Yampolsky translation, p. 135): "Meditation itself is the substance of wisdom; wisdom itself is the function of meditation."

56. It is sometimes claimed that the doctrines of *śūnyatā, nairātmya,* and the like were developed by the Mahāyāna phase of Buddhist thought, but they can be found in the early canonical texts. For example, in the *Saṃyutta-Nikāya* IV (*Saḷāyatana-Vagga,* 54), Ānanda asks the Buddha: "Lord, it is said that the world is *suñña* [= śūnya, "void"], the world is *suñña.* But Lord, in what respect is the world called *suñña?*" The Buddha answers, "Ānanda, as it is void of self or anything pertaining to self, therefore it is said, 'The world is void.'"

In that same *Nikāya,* III, p. 167, Sariputta says that a virtuous monk should consider the five aggregates as void and without self. Rahula, "Vijñaptimātratā Philosophy," p. 119, refers also to the *Suttanipāta,* verse 1119, wherein the Buddha tells Mogharāja to see the world as "void" by removing the idea of self. There are numerous other passages in which *Śūnyatā* is mentioned by the Buddha. Moreover, *nairātmya* and *śūnyatā* are interchangeable terms in the early canonical texts for signifying the idea of void, without self. Neither Nāgārjuna nor Asaṅga were inventing new doctrines. They were simply clarifying and "expanding" (the literal meaning of *vaipulya,* which characterizes a Mahāyāna treatise) ancient doctrines.

57. Nāgārjuna is revered as saint, scholar, philosopher, and mystic of Indian Buddhism. He is known as the "discoverer" of numerous Mahāyāna scriptures and as offering through his own compositions perhaps the most thoroughgoing critical analyses of *śūnyatā*. His *Mūlamādhyamikakārikā* came to serve as the fundamental treatise of the Mādhymaka school.

58. Bu-ston's *History* (Book I, p. 8) says, referring to the Buddha: "He has revealed (His) Doctrine in all its (three) forms." These three "Turnings of the Wheel" *(dharmacakrapravartana;* Tib. *chos-kyi-'khor-lo-bskor-ba)* are described in detail in the *Saṃdhinirmocana* (Lamotte: 85, 206).

59. There is usually a derogatory tone associated with the term "hīnayāna," rendered most often as "lesser" *(hīna)* "vehicle" *(yāna).* However, I am using it here in complete agreement with a statement advanced by Robert Thurman in his "Buddhist Hermeneutics," p. 37: "I use 'Hīnayāna' here to designate the teachings aiming at self-liberation from suffering by separate individuals, philosophically subdivided into eighteen schools during the centuries after Sākyamuni's death. 'Theravāda' is not serviceable for this purpose, as it represents only one of these eighteen schools, being the Pali form of Sanskrit *Sthāviravāda*. . . . I mean "individual" (not "inferior") by 'Hīna-' and 'universal' (not 'superior') by 'Mahā' of Mahāyāna. The former aims at individual liberation, not stressing the cultivation of love and compassion *(maitrīkarunā).* The latter aims at universal liberation, heavily stressing those virtues, but also including the necessity for individual liberation at the same time."

60. For example, see A. K. Chatterjee's *The Yogācāra Idealism,* p. 2. Other characterizations of the Three Turnings can be found in Stcherbatsky's *The Conception of Buddhist Nirvāṇa,* pp. 2–3 and in his *Buddhist Logic,* I, 3–14; also Dutt's *Buddhist Sects in India,* pp. 235–36.

61. Some scholars have attempted to answer the "problem" of the ordering of the last two Turnings by drawing analogy from developments within

Western philosophy. An example is provided by the opening statement of Professor Kalupahana's chapter on "Yogācāra Idealism" in his *Buddhist Philosophy: A Historical Analysis,* p. 142: "Just as the 'critical philosophy' of Immanuel Kant paved the way for Hegelian Idealism, even so the critical philosophy of Nāgārjuna may be said to have contributed to the systematized form of absolute Idealism of Vasubandhu, although Idealism as such was not unknown earlier." Assuming that the Mādhyamika represents the highest advance of Mahāyāna philosophy, such scholars feel the need to justify its middle position within the ordering of the traditional schema.

62. Some scholars, of course, often warned against such dichotomizing, notably D. T. Suzuki, Alex Wayman, Walpola Rahula, and Gadjin Nagao. In his "President's Address" to the First Conference of the International Association of Buddhist Studies (New York, September 15, 1978), Gadjin Nagao stated: "The gap between the Mādhyamika and the Vijñanavāda traditions must be bridged, because the Mādhyamikas and the Vijñanavādins were not, from the beginning, two antithetical schools, as is usually assumed."

63. These three stages are not unlike those in an old Zen saying: "First there is a mountain, then there isn't, then there is." The last "mountain" is experienced by the Zen practitioner in a manner which is *qualitatively* different from the first. Indeed, the perception of voidness and things together is the ultimate union *(yoga)* wherein one realizes directly the ultimate mode of existence of all things.

64. Here the traditional warning, most often voiced by Mādhyamikas, must be heeded. Voidness is not itself an entity, and it is a grave mistake to hypostatize it. Hence the Mādhyamikas teach *śūnyatāśūnayatā,* the "voidness of voidness." Asaṅga's stance with regard to *śūnyatā* is voiced more positively in order to allay fears of complete nihilism. Thus he states in the *Tattvārtha* chapter: "Now, how is voidness rightly conceptualized? . . . whatever remains in that place one knows as it really is, that 'here' there is an existent." *Śūnyatā* is therefore treated as an existent by the Yogācāra, but it is important to see that by this characterization, Asaṅga wishes to assert that *śūnyatā* exists as the ultimate *mode* of existence of all things (and not itself as an existent thing).

65. It is known that Asaṅga wrote commentaries on some of the *Prajñāpāramitā* literature. His commentary on the *Vajracchedikāsūtra* is among those collected by G. Tucci in *Minor Buddhist Texts, Part I.* Moreover, the *Heart Sūtra* is often referred to as a Yogācāra scripture.

66. Most of Asaṅga's writing can be seen as relating more to practice than to doctrine strictly speaking. The *Bodhisattvabhūmi* is a good case in point.

NOTES TO THE INTRODUCTION

According to mKhas-grub-rje's *Fundamentals of the Buddhist Tantras* (Lessing and Wayman translation, p. 99): "The *tattva* chapter of the *Bodhisattvabhūmi* teaches doctrine, while the remaining chapters teach practice. Apart from that one chapter, all the others, which set forth the practice, constitute a commentary on the general purport of the *Mahāyāna sūtra* section." It is therefore to none other than the *Tattva* chapter herein translated that we should look to get an idea of Asaṅga's philosophical position, especially as regards his views on the Mahāyāna doctrine of ultimate reality.

67. This language is borrowed from Stephan Beyer's *The Cult of Tārā,* especially pp. 92 ff. On p. 92 Beyer states: "Much of Buddhist 'ontological psychology' is an attempt to explain in historical terms why we make a systematic epistemological error in our apprehension of the world, why we attribute to it a solidity that in fact it does not possess."

68. Robert Thurman, "Buddhist Hermeneutics," *Journal of the American Academy of Religion,* 46 (1978), 27.

69. This is in complete agreement with Thurman's assessment, ibid.

70. Beyer, *The Cult of Tārā,* p. 95, renders this passage somewhat differently. He writes: "When something does not exist someplace, one sees truly that it is 'empty' with regard to it; and when something remains there, one knows that it is really there." Beyer continues: "When nonreality is emptied of subject and object, what remains—what is 'really there'—is Emptiness." Again, for Asaṅga śūnyatā is the formal structure of relative existence, the ultimate mode of that existence.

71. See his *Studies in the Laṅkāvatāra Sūtra,* p. 170.

72. One is inclined to agree with the Reverend Walpola Rahula's assessment found in his "Vijñaptimātratā Philosophy in the Yogācāra System and Some Wrong Notions," p. 118, that far from founding new philosophical schools, such thinkers were but "expounding the old teaching with their own new interpretations, explanations, arguments and theories, according to their own genius, ability, knowledge and experience. . . . Their contribution to Buddhism lay not in giving it a new philosophy but providing, in fascinatingly different ways, brilliant new interpretations and explanations of the old philosophy."

73. For example, A. K. Chatterjee's work, *The Yogācāra Idealism,* is replete with the phrase "The Yogācāra holds that consciousness is the sole reality." The statement seems to have become the catch phrase for characterizing the philosophical position of the school as a whole. Other examples can be found in T. R. V. Murti's *Central Philosophy of Buddhism,* pp. 105 and 197, and E. J. Thomas' *History of Buddhist Thought,* p. 233.

74. By "two varying streams" I do not mean the generally accepted divisions of the Yogācāra into the so-called (1) early idealists and (2) later logicians. To be sure, Diṅnāga, who was a pupil of Vasubandhu, according to Buddhist tradition, did establish a new wing of Yogācāra which laid great stress on logic and which diverges at important points from the positions of Asaṅga and Vasubandhu. However, my concern in the present study is to attempt to delineate the two streams of thought *within* the so-called "idealistic" phase of the Yogācāra. My contention is that while later Yogācārins like Dharmapāla (6th century) employ key terms associated with the school in a way that seems to deny the existence of external entities altogether, the earliest doctors of the school—Asaṅga, Vasubandhu, and Sthiramati—do not.

75. For an extremely valuable treatment of this subject, see Yoshifumi Ueda, "Two Main Streams of Thought in Yogācāra Philosophy."

76. Ibid., pp. 156–62.

77. Dharmapāla's writings were translated into Chinese by Hsüan-tsang as the *Ch'eng wei shih lun,* which is now available to us in French through the impressive translating efforts of La Vallée Poussin. See his *Vijñaptimātratā-siddhi—La Siddhi de Hiuan-tsang.* Takakusu, in *The Essentials of Buddhist Philosophy,* pp. 83–84, points out that following the death of Vasubandhu, there were three further lines of development of the Yogācāra: (1) the line of Dignāga, Agotra, and Dharmapāla, whose center of transmission was Nālandā University; (2) the line of Guṇamati and Sthiramati, whose seat seems to have been Valābhi University; and (3) the line of Nanda, "whose tenet was followed by Paramārtha."

Though listed first, Dharmapāla's line was not historically the earliest to reach China. Paramārtha's translations of the works of Maitreya, Asaṅga, and Vasubandhu found their way there long before Hsüan-tsang introduced the "later" tradition of Yogācāra thought through his translation of Dharmapāla's great synthesis. However, this tradition is the one best known by contemporary scholars, while the others are much less so.

78. This procedure is both stressed and put to good use by Lambert Schmithausen; see, e.g., "On the Problem of the Relation of Spiritual Practice and Philosophical Theory in Buddhism."

79. Though explicated by Asaṅga some 1500 years ago, the notion of *ālaya* is in fact not very different from modern day psychological theories of the unconscious. It refers to a subliminal, subconscious repository of cognitions that functions as a sort of clearinghouse where all mental events *(dharmas)* are processed. To quote Schmithausen, ibid., p. 237, "The objective contents of this ālayavijñāna consists [sic] of a mental image of the whole

world and is determined by the former good and bad deeds *(karman)* of the respective living being. Thus, the whole world, especially the outer world, is only a subjective mental production of each being."

This model is consistent with the Yogācāra's "conceptualization-only" *(vijñaptimātra)* theory, which declares that ordinary cognitions do not actually "reach" outside objects. Rather they are just mental reflections, object-like mental images *(vijñapti)*. Of course it must be noted, in Schmithausen's words (ibid., pp. 237–38), "that for the Yogācāras even this manifold universe of fluctuating mental factors is only an imperfect or preliminary level of reality. In mystical intuition one can become aware of a deeper reality constituted by the so-called 'Suchness' or 'True Essence.' "

80. E. J. Thomas, *History of Buddhist Thought,* p. 233. See also, p. 234, where Thomas writes: "All things having been explained as mind or consciousness, the ultimate reality is then interpreted as the fundamental store-consciousness."

81. See the *Abhidharmasamuccaya,* Pradhan edition, pp. 11 ff.

82. *Citta* and *ālaya* are also treated as identical in the *Saṃdhinirmocanasūtra* (Lamotte trans., pp. 55, 185) and throughout the *Laṅkāvatārasūtra.*

83. See *Abhidharmasamuccaya,* Pradhan ed., pp. 11 ff.

84. As Schmithausen notes ("On the Problem of the Relation of Spiritual Practice and Philosophical Theory in Buddhism," p. 244), the *Daśabhūmikasūtra* antedates both the *Bodhisattvabhūmi* and the *Saṃdhinirmocana sūtra:* "This sūtra is referred to already in the *Bodhisattvabhūmi* chapter of the *Yogācārabhūmi,* and was translated into Chinese by Dharmarakṣa as early as the last decade of the 3rd Century A.D. Thus it is doubtlessly older than the *Saṃdhinirmocanasūtra* which in fact, also in the 8th chapter, adopts its theory of the ten stages of a Bodhisattva."

85. Buddhist cosmology recognizes three realms, or "worlds" *(tridhātu),* known as the desire realm *(kāmadhātu),* the material or form realm *(rūpadhātu),* and the immaterial or formless realm *(arūpyadhātu).*

86. Wayman, in "The Meanings of the Term Cittamātra," p. 1, notes that "the Pure Land tradition of Japanese Buddhism holds that Nāgārjuna composed the *Daśabhūmika-sūtra;* and it would not detract from this tradition if that celebrated passage about mind-only can be understood in a Mādhyamika way; while we also know that Vasubandhu wrote a commentary in the Yogācāra way on the *Daśabhūmika-sūtra.*"

87. Ibid., p. 1. Wayman cites Tsoṅ-kha-pa's commentary on Candrakīrti's *Madhyamakāvatāra* as the source for this interpretation.

88. See Schmithausen, "On the Problem of the Relation . . . ," p. 246.

89. Ibid., pp. 246–47.

90. While the final paragraph of this quotation shows that the *Bhadrapālasūtra* does go on to "extend" the notion of *cittamātra* to all phenomena, Schmithausen, p. 247, duly notes that its "thesis of universal idealism originated from the *generalization* of a situation observed in the case of objects visualized in meditative concentration, i.e., in the context of *spiritual* practice."

91. *Ālambana* refers to the mental support of cognition, or the object cognized; *pratibimba* means "reflected image." In meditative contexts, *ālambana* is equivalent to *nimitta,* literally "sign" or "mark," which is applied both to the objective and the subjective ideal of meditation. Technically speaking, there are three stages or levels of *nimitta:* First, the "preliminary sign" *(parikamma nimitta)* employed in the preliminary practice. This usually refers to a concrete object of ordinary experience. Second, the "leaving sign" *(uggaha nimitta)* which is an exact copy of the object, now internalized and presented vividly to the mind. When this level has been grasped, there is no longer need of the concrete meditation object, or device. Lastly, there is the so-called "after-image" or counterpart sign *(paṭibhāga nimitta).* At this stage of the practice, the meditator's concentration is said to have divested the image of its "limitations" and "faults" *(kasiṇa dosa)* and the sign is transformed into a concept, an abstract idea (which nevertheless remains individualized, since it is still connected to a particular object). In this final stage, Mahāthera *(Buddhist Meditation,* p. 145) tells us, the after-image "is no longer presented to the senses or to the cognitive faculty as a concrete object. But this image remains in the mind as an emblematic representation of the whole quality or element that it symbolizes." It is this last form of the meditative object which Yogācārins refer to—in meditative contexts—as being "wholly mind" *(cittamātra)* or "wholly conceptualization" *(vijñaptimātra).* The description of the transformation of the meditative device presumes the reality (and externality) of the preliminary sign; and thus the reality of ordinary objects is not called into question.

92. Schmithausen, "On the Problem of the Relation . . . ," p. 240.

93. Ibid., p. 238. Referring to the *Yogācārabhūmi,* Schmithausen notes: "In this text, as far as I can see, the idealistic-spiritualistic philosophy of later Yogācāras and its characteristic terms, *vijñaptimātra* and *cittamātra,* are not yet traceable. I found only one passage in which the text asserts that only the mind *(cittamātra)* exists really. But it is an opponent who is speaking in this passage, and moreover the statement is not, as usually, directed against

the existence of real objects outside the mind but merely against the opinion that, besides the mind, we have to accept the existence of emotional and volitional mental factors."

94. See Lamotte's *La Somme du Grande Véhicule,* I, 93–94.

95. The identity of meditation and wisdom is stressed most often in Ch'an, or Zen, texts. A good example is provided by the famed *Platform Sūtra* (of the Sixth Patriarch), Yampolsky translation, p. 135:

> Good friends, my teaching of the Dharma takes meditation *(ting)* and wisdom *(hui)* as its basis. Never under any circumstances say mistakenly that meditation and wisdom are different; they are a unity, not two things. Meditation itself is the substance of wisdom; wisdom itself is the function of meditation. At the very moment when there is wisdom, then meditation exists in wisdom; at the very moment when there is meditation, then wisdom exists in meditation. Good friends, this means that meditation and wisdom are alike. Students, be careful not to say that meditation gives rise to wisdom, or that wisdom gives rise to meditation, or that meditation and wisdom are different from each other.

It seems clear that the Yogācāra recognized this identity and made it the center of its teaching. As Conze remarks in *Buddhist Thought in India,* p. 253,

> Asaṅga appeals to the experience of transic meditation. Our empirical mental processes are not all on the same level, and some are less estranged from ultimate truth than others. In ordinary sense-perception the estrangement has gone very far, but not so in transic meditation, because 'the concentrated see things as they really are.'

And again as Schmithausen notes, "On the Problem of the Relation . . . ," p. 247, that the Yogācāra's so-called philosophical position of idealism "originated from the generalization of a situation observed in the case of objects visualized in meditative concentration. . . ."

96. Wayman, "The Yogācāra Idealism", in *Philosophy East and West,* 15, no. 1 (1965), 69.

97. See Rahula, "Vijñaptimātratā Philosophy . . . ," p. 122.

98. Schmithausen, "On the Problem of the Relation . . . ," pp. 247–48.

99. In *The Dawn of Tantra,* p. 12, for example, Chogyam Trungpa Tulku makes the following statement: "The idea of tantra as continuity connects this inquiry with the philosophy of the Yogacara since this early Indian school of Buddhist philosophy was instrumental in developing the idea of tantra."

100. Wayman in "The Meanings of the Term Cittamātra", p. 8, also cites

this verse, rendering the initial line as "There is nothing manifested outside, for the mind manifests the multiplicity."

101. The term *neyārtha* is used to refer to Buddhist teachings which are given in terms of relative truth requiring further interpretation. It is best rendered "indirect" or "interpretable" meaning.

102. This description by Warder, *Indian Buddhism,* p. 432.

103. See Suzuki's preface to the *Laṅkāvatārasūtra,* p. xi.

104. Wayman notes this in "The Meanings of the Term Cittamātra," p. 8: "the Laṅkāvatāra has the feature of identifying the *ālayavijñana* with the *tathāgatagarbha,* which is not found in the Asaṅga-Vasubandhu school." The notion of the *tathāgatagarbha* posits the theory that all sentient beings have the potentiality of Buddhahood. Its chief scriptural authority is the *Śrīmālā sūtra,* which is said to have helped inspire the *Laṅkāvatārasūtra.* The points of divergence between the notion of *tathāgatagarbha* and that of the *ālayavijñāna* are explicated in detail in Alex and Hideko Wayman's translation, *The Lion's Roar of Queen Śrīmālā.*

105. Edward Conze in *Buddhist Thought in India,* pp. 252–53, eloquently expands upon this intentional usage:

> (Their) assertion about the non-existence of objects is, however, a soteriological device and its main function consists in acting as the first step of a meditation on the perverted views. . . . The bare statement denying the existence of external objects belongs to a fairly low and preliminary stage of realization, and though it may loom large in the philosophical discussions with rival schools, it is no more than a stepping stone to better things. The real point of asserting the unreality of an object *qua* object is to further the withdrawal from all external objective supports *(ālambana),* both through the increasing introversion of transic meditation and through the advance on the higher stages of a Bodhisattva's career when, as we saw, no longer tied to an object he acts out of the free spontaneity of his inner being. For a long time, i.e., until he has overcome the last vestige of an object, the subject *(grāhaka)* must seem more real to the Bodhisattva than the object. But at the very last stage of his journey he comes to realize that with the final collapse of the object also the separate subject has ceased to be and that also thought and its concomitants, in so far as they take an object, do not constitute an ultimate fact.

106. Cited in Wayman, "The Meanings of the Term Cittamātra," p. 9. The verse quoted by Tsoṅ-kha-pa is number 123 in the *Laṅkāvatāra*'s Chapter II.

107. Kalupahana, *Buddhist Philosophy: A Historical Analysis,* p. 143.

108. Summarizing this intentional usage on the part of Vasubandhu,

Wayman, in his "The Yogācāra Idealism (Review Article)," p. 68, gives a similar appraisal. He says with regard to the *Viṃśatikā* and *Triṃśikā:* "In the former work, Vasubandhu stresses ideation-only *(vijñaptimātra)* because he is setting forth the process of world illusion created by the *Madhyāntavibhaṅga's* 'imagination of unreality'. . . . In the latter work, Vasubandhu again stresses ideation-only because he is setting forth the removal of the world illusion."

109. All the following verses are translated from the Chinese version of Hsüan-tsang by Wing-tsit Chan and are found in Radhakrishnan and Moore's *A Sourcebook in Indian Philosophy,* pp. 333–37.

110. It is hoped that the foregoing has shed some light on this contention. It is interesting that in Wayman's "The Meanings of the Term Cittamātra," p. 6, Masaaki Hattori is quoted as saying, "the developed Yogācāra school stems from the Vijñaptimātratā after Vasubandhu and in this later school there is definitely a denial of the external object."

111. For example, see the use of *tattva* in this way in the Sāṁkhya and Yoga schools of the six orthodox Hindu philosophical systems. The Sāṁkhya speaks of the twenty-four elements of reality as distinct and objective *tattvas,* in reference to the self *(puruṣa),* taken as the twenty-fifth *tattva.* Even the heterodox Jaina system employs the concept of multiple *tattvas* in expounding its system. The Buddhist tantras often speak of *tattvas* in this multiple sense, as for example, when the *Tattva-saṃgraha* lists thirty-seven *tattvas* or "reals" of its system, which it further identifies with various deities, *mūdras,* etc. For more detailed explanation of these various systems and their uses of the term, see K. Bhattacharya's *Studies in Philosophy,* vol. I, especially pp. 158–250; Lessing and Wayman, *mKhas-grub-rje's Fundamentals of the Buddhist Tantras;* and Radhakrishnan and Moore, *A Sourcebook in Indian Philosophy.*

112. Wittgenstein, *Philosophical Investigations,* p. 2.

113. Asaṅga's exegesis of this chapter devotes the bulk of its discussion to the workings of *vikalpa* and concludes by praising the state of *nirvikalpa jñāna,* i.e., "knowledge completely freed of discursive thought."

114. *Bodhisattva* literally means "one whose whole being *(sattva)* is intent on ultimate enlightenment *(bodhi).* Strictly speaking, then, there is no limitation associated with the term as to the sex of such a one. This is not to say, however, that Buddhism is non-sexist. In fact, the scriptures of early and later Buddhism profess the general assumption that the highest goal can only be attained by men and that women who desire this goal must first be reincarnated in male form in order to obtain it.

NOTES TO THE INTRODUCTION

Given the cultural context of sixth-century B.C. India as well as the importance of celibacy to the early Buddhist monastic organization, it is not surprising that women would have been devalued. Coomaraswamy *(Buddha and the Gospel of Buddhism,* p. 160) cites the following excerpt from the early sūtras:

> 'Master,' says Ānanda, 'how shall we behave before women?'—'You should shun their gaze, Ānanda' —'But if we see them, master, what then are we to do?' —'Not speak to them, Ānanda.' —'But if we do speak to them, what then?' —'Then you must watch over yourselves, Ānanda.'

I. B. Horner in her *Women Under Primitive Buddhism* devotes an entire chapter to Ānanda and Gautama Buddha's relationship to women (see esp. pp. 295–312). Ānanda, perhaps Gautama's favorite disciple, is shown in the scriptures to be a chief advocate for women, and honor falls to him for having pushed for the admission of women to the Buddhist order. Mahāprajāpatī, the Buddha's aunt, became the first nun or *bhikkhuni.* Previous to her admission, Ānanda had queried, "Are women competent, Revered Sir . . . to attain the fruit of conversion, to attain the fruit of once-returning . . . of never-returning, to attain to Arhatship?" The Buddha did not deny their competence, but predicted that, as a result of founding a women's order, his doctrine would not abide long in India. But women *were* admitted to the Buddhist order, and they did cultivate the Buddhist monastic way. Many attained to Arhatship and to Nirvāṇa as attested to in their "songs of triumph," the *Therīgāthā*, translated by C. A. F. Rhys Davids as *Psalms of the Sisters.*

On the other hand, the scriptures show, as Coomaraswamy, p. 163, points out, that the Buddha had a number of devout (and wealthy) laywomen followers also. Among the list of such illustrious women of early Buddhism are: Khemā, Uppalavannā, Patācārā, Bhaddā, Kisā Gotamī, Dhammadinnā, and Visākhā.

When we come to the scriptures of the Mahāyāna with its more universal outlook, one might expect to find less explicit disparagement of the female sex, but this is not generally the case. For example, the *Lotus Sūtra* (H. Kern, trans., chapter XI, "Apparition of a Stupa," p. 252) records:

> Then the venerable Sāriputra said to that daughter of Sāgara, the Nāga-king; Thou hast conceived the idea of enlightenment, young lady of good family, without sliding back, and art gifted with immense wisdom, but supreme, perfect enlightenment is not easily won. It may happen, sister, that a woman displays an unflagging energy, performs good works for many thou-

sands of aeons, and fulfils the six perfect virtues (Pāramitās), but as yet there is no example of her having reached Buddhaship, and that because a woman cannot occupy the five ranks, viz. 1. the rank of Brahma; 2. the rank of Indra; 3. the rank of a chief guardian of the four quarters; 4. the rank of Kakravartin; 5. the rank of a Bodhisattva incapable of sliding back.

Kern adds in a note to this passage: "All these beings [i.e. of the list of five] are in Sanskrit of masculine gender; hence their rank cannot be taken by beings having feminine names."

In another passage from the *Lotus* (Hurvitz trans., Ch. 23, "Former Affairs of the Bodhisattva Medicine King," p. 300), we find:

If a woman, hearing this Chapter of the Former Affairs of the Bodhisattva Medicine King, can accept and keep it, she shall put an end to her female body, and shall never again receive one.

The *Vimalakīrtinirdeśasūtra,* in an episode which bears close affinity to the passage immediately following the one just cited from the *Lotus,* a goddess instructs Śāriputra that a female form is no hindrance to comprehending the ultimate, void, nature of reality. However, the thrust of the passage is that reality transcends all distinctions, including those associated with a given sex. It reads (Thurman, trans., p. 61):

Śāriputra: Goddess, what prevents you from transforming yourself out of your female state?

Goddess: Although I have sought my "female state" for these twelve years, I have not yet found it. Reverend Śāriputra, if a magician were to incarnate a woman by magic, would you ask her, 'What prevents you from transforming yourself out of your female state?'

Śāriputra: No! Such a woman would not really exist, so what would there be to transform?

Goddess: Just so, reverend Śāriputra, all things do not really exist.

The *Śrī-Mālā sūtra,* which the Waymans (p. 2) judge to be "a Mahāyāna outgrowth of the later Mahāsāṅghika" composed in the third century A.D., gives us a positive picture of female capabilities. According to the Waymans' assessment (p. 36):

When the *Śrī-Mālā* allows that a good daughter of the family, by renouncing possessions (having previously renounced body and life force) is endowed with uninterrupted, permanent, and inconceivable merits that are unshared by other sentient beings, it apparently makes her equivalent in the terminology of other scriptures to a Bodhisattva of the Tenth Stage.

This is about as exalted a status as can be pointed to among the Buddhist scriptures. With later developments in practice, especially the later emphasis on tantra, there is a shift upwards with respect to how women are esteemed. For example, four of the famed "eighty-four mahāsiddhas" are women. Yet for the most part it remains true throughout the history of Buddhism that the woman is expected to show deference to the man.

I cannot argue that the Buddha or Asaṅga took up the "woman's cause." There is clear evidence that they did not. However, it is equally true that were the chief teachings of Buddhism comprehended and put into practice, there would be little need to take up such a mantle. As the Goddess in the *Vimalakīrti sūtra* tells Śāriputra (Thurman, trans., p. 62): "the Buddha said, 'In all things, there is neither male nor female'."

115. *Tathāgata* is one of the chief epithets of the Buddha, especially in Mahāyāna texts. The term is ambiguous; it may be viewed either as the compound, *tathā* + *gata* and rendered the "One thus gone," or as *tathā* + *agata,* the "One thus come" to Enlightenment.

116. "Path of Instruction" = *sikṣā-mārga. Sikṣa* refers to the "threefold training" set down in early Buddhism (and upon which Buddhaghoṣa's *Visuddhimagga*'s three divisions are based). The three trainings are those in (1) *śīla,* or moral discipline; (2) *samādhi* (or *citta),* contemplation and absorption; and (3) *prajñā,* insight. The threefold trainings are fundamental to both the Hīnayāna and the Mahāyāna.

117. Specific details regarding these sūtras are given in the commentary accompanying the present translation. It is interesting to note here again that of the three texts quoted in the chapter by Asaṅga, two are early scriptures of the Hīnayāna tradition. The *Bhavasaṃkrāntisūtra,* though classed by the *Mahāvyutpatti* (no. 1379) as a Mahāyāna text, is noted there to be one of the earliest Mahāyāna scriptures. Hence, Asaṅga, far from seeking to present a new philosophical system, clearly evidences by including these particular quotations both his devotion to his early education and training in a Hīnayāna sect, and his firm conviction that he is but reiterating the Buddha's own original teaching as set down in the early canonical literature.

The Chapter on Knowing Reality

[I]

What is knowledge of reality? Concisely, there are two sorts: (1) that sort which consists of [knowing] the noumenal aspect *(yathāvadbhāvikatā)* of dharmas, or the true state of dharmas as they are in themselves *(bhūtatā)*; and (2) that sort which consists of [knowing] the phenomenal aspect *(yāvadbhāvikatā)* of dharmas, as they are in totality *(sarvatā)*. In short, knowledge of reality should be understood as [knowledge of] "dharmas as they are, and as they are in totality."

Both the types of knowledge referred to above are those types belonging to the Buddhas. Hence, Asaṅga begins the chapter by defining that superior *(uttama)* knowledge to which the bodhisattva should aspire.

The use of *sarvatā* (Tib. *tham cad ñid)* in reference to the second type of knowledge, by suggesting the idea of cognition which is all-encompassing, is in keeping with one of the common epithets of a Buddha, *sarvajña*, "omniscient." Taking the two types together, then, a Buddha knows directly the essential nature *(svabhāva)* of each individual dharma in itself, as it really is (type 1 above); and such a one knows simultaneously the entire *(sarvatā)* realm of dharmas *(dharmadhātu)* as a whole (type 2). He has direct knowledge of all phenomena *(sarvatā)* and their mode of being *(bhūtatā)*. As we are told later in the chapter, for an "Enlightened One," the two types of knowledge are in fact one knowledge, i.e., the knowledge of the void *(śūnya)* nature of all dharmas. From both the noumenal and phenomenal points of view, the essential nature of all dharmas is the same *(sama)*, namely voidness *(śūnyatā)*.

Further, knowledge of reality may be given a fourfold analysis, as follows:

(1) what is universally accepted by ordinary beings;
(2) what is universally accepted by reason, or logic;
(3) that which is the sphere of cognitive activity *(jñānagocara)* completely purified of the obscurations of defilement *(kleśāvaraṇa)*; and
(4) that which is the sphere of cognitive activity completely purified of obscurations to the knowable *(jñeyāvaraṇa)*.

Having described the highest type of knowledge—that to be sought after by the bodhisattva—Asaṅga now begins anew, to trace the various kinds of knowledge possessed by beings at different stages of ability and accomplishment. He tells us that different types of cognition of reality are possessed by four classes of beings: (1) ordinary beings, (2) logicians, (3) Buddhist Hīnayāna practitioners (i.e., śrāvakas and pratyekabuddhas), and (4) Mahāyāna practitioners (i.e., Buddhas and bodhisattvas). This same fourfold analysis is adhered to in other works by Asaṅga as well as by later doctors of the Yogācāra who follow the main lines of Asaṅga's original thought.

Asaṅga states clearly at the end of the chapter that the first two of these four types of knowledge are inferior, the third is middling, and only the fourth is superior *(uttama)*.

There follows a brief description of the first and second kinds of knowledge. Ordinary beings, we are told, perceive only the phenomenal aspect of objects. Their knowledge is conditioned by the foregone conclusion that entities exist just as they are expressed, i.e., that names accurately characterize the nature of the things named. The knowledge possessed by logicians differs from this type in that logicians' knowledge of things results from a more careful analysis—albeit still only of dharmas' phenomenal aspects—which uses the standard logical proofs.

> Of these four, the first may be defined as follows: The shared opinion of all worldly beings—because their minds are involved with and proceed according to signs *(saṃketa)* and conventions *(saṃvṛti)*, out of habit *(saṃstava)*—with respect to any "given thing" *(vastu)*, is like so: "Earth is earth alone, and not fire." And as with earth, just so fire, water, wind, forms, sounds, smells, tastes, tactiles, food, drink, conveyance, clothes, ornaments, utensils, incense, garlands, ointments, dance, song, music, illumination, sexual intercourse, fields, shops, household objects, happiness, and suffering are viewed accordingly. "This is suffering, not happiness." "This is happiness, not suffering." In short, "This is this, and not that." And likewise, "This is this, and not any other."

ON KNOWING REALITY

> Whatever given thing is taken hold of and becomes established for all ordinary beings owing merely to their own discursive thought *(vikalpa),* by means of associations *(saṃjñā)* arising one after another in the sphere of foregone conclusions, without having been pondered, without having been weighed and measured, and without having been investigated, that is said to be the reality which is universally accepted by ordinary beings, or which is established by worldly consent.

Vastu in this context refers, as the Tibetan equivalent *dṅos po* suggests, to any perceivable or tangible object of experience. The closest approximation to *vastu* used in this sense is the ordinary English term "thing." It is translated here as "given thing" because there is also the idea of its being a specific thing "at hand" or "in the mind," i.e., available for ostensive definition, at least to oneself, as Asaṅga's closing statement to the section indicates: "This is this, and not any other."

Saṃstava is a key term here and refers to a view that has been acquired through repeated use and exercise. It is habit, performed automatically and without prior investigation. Paul Wilfred O'Brien, in his "A Chapter on Reality from the *Madhyāntavibhāgaśāstra,*" pp. 231–32, cites two sources which further define the term: (1) the *P'u-sa-shan-chieh-ching,* T. 30, 1582, p. 986b: "When an object, through its name having been transmitted from of old by the whole world, is known spontaneously and not as the result of [repeated] accumulated practice, this is called reality established through common consent"; and (2) Hsien-yang, T. 31, p. 507b: "Reality established through common consent is the conventional nature commonly postulated with reference to objects by all mankind by means of an intellectual knowledge acquired from custom."

A proper understanding of the detrimental character of *saṃstava,* especially with regard to our ordinary use of language, is one of the chief concerns of the chapter, first because a key part of Asaṅga's methodological approach to analyzing knowledge of reality—both here and in his exegesis—is the careful examination of the relationship between names (generated, learned, and passed on through habit and custom) and the things to which these are attached. It is precisely because of our "habitual certainty" with regard to language usage that we conclude that we know what a thing is when we know its name. To indicate the error of such a view, Asaṅga tells us that this characteristic tendency marks the inferior type of knowledge about reality. Indeed, in his exegesis, he defines imaginary (i.e., completely false, *parikalpita)* nature solely in terms of this common practice with respect to language usage. There he states: (19b.8) "What is the imaginary nature? It is that nature arising from name and sign [Tib. *brda,* here = "object"] and because of which there is subsequently the attaching of a designation." Hence, an alternate rendering for *parikalpita* nature is "*imputed* nature." Moreover, close examination of the true relationship between names and things may be used as a vehicle for guiding us to a proper understanding of the essential nature of both these—and thereby, by extension, to the essential nature of all dharmas.

What is that reality universally accepted by reason *(yukti)*? It is that which is known from the personal eloquence of those at the stage of being governed by reason, who are learned in the meaning of logical principles, and who have intelligence, reasoning power, and skill in investigation. Also, it is that knowledge arising in ordinary beings which is based on the authority of those engaged in investigation, namely, the proofs *(pramāṇa)* of the logicians: direct perception, inference, and the testimony of trustworthy persons. That is the sphere of well-analyzed knowledge wherein the knowable given thing is proven and established by demonstration-and-proof reason. That is said to be the reality which is universally accepted by reason.

What is the reality which is the sphere of cognitive activity completely purified of the obscurations of defilement? It is that domain and sphere of cognitive activity attained by putting an end to the outflows *(āsrava)*, which is the "putting an end to the outflows" of all the śrāvakas and pratyekabuddhas, as well as that mundane knowledge which puts an end to the outflows at some future time. That reality is said to be the sphere of cognitive activity that is completely purified of the obscurations of defilement. When knowledge becomes purified of the obscurations of defilement, i.e., of those three mental supports [the three defilements], one dwells in nonobscuration. Therefore, it is called reality which is the sphere of cognitive activity completely purified of the obscurations of defilement.

Asaṅga now addresses himself to the two classes of Hīnayāna practitioners, i.e., the *śrāvakas* (lit. the "hearers"), those monks who adhere strictly to the literal sense of Gautama's discourses, and seek Nirvāṇa as their ultimate goal, and the *pratyekabuddhas* (seeking lit. "Buddhahood for oneself alone"), Buddhist practitioners who, having heard the doctrine, retire into complete retreat and isolation from worldly affairs. Even though pratyekabuddhas are exceptional beings, possessing great powers of energy, will, and concentration, they too seek only Nirvāṇa. Asaṅga describes their knowledge of reality as "middling," i.e., as superior to ordinary beings' and logicians', but inferior to that knowledge possessed by the Buddhas and bodhisattvas.

The śrāvakas and pratyekabuddhas are said to possess a clearer knowledge of reality owning to the fact that they have rid themselves of the defiling emotions of greed, hatred, and delusion. According to Buddhist tradition, these three "defilements" *(kleśas)* generate the whole cycle of saṃsāra.

Saṃsāra (Tib. *'kor ba)* refers to the round, or wheel, of mental and physical existence, running rampant, ever changing, marked most notably by the characteristic of *duḥkha,* suffering or misery.

Lust, hatred, and delusion *(rāga-dveṣa-moha;* Tib. *'dod-chags, źe-sdaṅ* and *gti-mug)* are the three fundamental, or "greater," defilements. In the famed Tibetan temple banners depicting saṃsāra, these three are depicted as a snake, a cock, and a boar, respectively, and drawn in the centermost hub of the "Wheel of Saṃsāra," suggesting that the three are the very basis of the "world of suffering."

Strictly speaking, *āsravas* (rendered here literally as "outflows") refers to what Dayal, *Bodhisattva Doctrine,* p. 109, calls "more metaphysical and fundamental sins and errors" than the kleśas, which he describes as "ordinary faults of character." The three primary āsravas (a fourth was added at a later period) were the outflows associated with sense-desire *(kām-āsrava)*, "becoming" or love of existence *(bhav-āsrava)*, and ignorance *(avidy-āsrava)*. Later times saw the addition of the outflow associated with speculative views or opinions *(dṛṣṭy-āsrava)*. The complete destruction of the āsravas *(āsrava-kṣaya)* represented the *summum bonum* of early Buddhist religious life and marked the attainment of arhatship. Again according to Dayal, p. 109, later leaders of the Hīnayāna and the Mahāyāna "quietly ignored the more difficult ideal of *āsrava-kṣaya*" considering it "too strenuous for ordinary monks."

This passage of Asaṅga's is unique in Buddhist literature because here the *āsravas* are clearly identified with the primary kleśas. Dayal argues strongly against identifying these with kleśas and cites the *Bodhisattvabhūmi* as the sole text wherein this identification is found. But clearly for Asaṅga those śrāvakas and pratyekabuddhas who have rid themselves of the kleśas have thereby rid themselves of the "outflows" as well. Having accomplished this, they are said to possess a knowledge of reality which is completely freed of the first of the two main veils, obstacles or "obscurations," to a perfected view of reality as it really is.

By "mundane knowledge" *(laukika jñāna)* Asaṅga presumably refers to knowledge of others in the worldly career, i.e., to certain lay practitioners who may reach this goal in the future, and perhaps even to non-Buddhists who practice another "way" which may nevertheless lead to this same result.

Moreover, what is that reality? The Four Noble Truths, namely: (1) suffering, (2) its origin, (3) its cessation, and (4) the path leading to its cessation. It is that knowledge which arises in those having clear comprehension who, after thorough investigation, arrive at the understanding of these Four Noble Truths. Further, it is the understanding of those truths on the part of those śrāvakas and pratyekabuddhas who have apprehended that there are only aggregates *(skandha-mātra)* [in what is commonly assumed to be a person] and who have not apprehended a self *(ātman)* as a separate entity apart from the aggregates. By means of insight *(prajñā)* properly applied to the arising and passing away of all dependently arisen *(pratītyasamutpanna),* conditioned states, clear vision *(darśana)* arises from the repetition of the view that "apart from the aggregates there is no 'person'."

Here Asaṅga lays out the path of practice by which the śrāvakas and pratyekabuddhas attain to knowledge completely purified of the obscurations of defilement. The practice is two-pronged, though it is performed concurrently. It involves continued study, investigation, and meditation upon the Four Noble Truths. Insight into the true purport of the truths is obtained by those practitioners who have penetrated and well understood the doctrine of dependent origination *(pratītyasamutpada).* Such understanding for śrāvakas and pratyekabuddhas arises, we are told, from the meditative "repetition of the view that apart from the aggregates there is no 'person.' "

In summary, Hīnayāna practitioners may attain a knowledge of reality which is completely untainted by greed, hatred, and delusion by fully comprehending the purport of the Four Noble Truths and by the direct realization of *ātmanairātmya,* i.e., that there is no actually existent "self" in the conglomerate of psychophysical elements we commonly think of as a "self," or as a "person" *(pudgala).*

> What is the reality which is the sphere of cognitive activity completely purified of the obscurations to the knowable? That which prevents knowledge of a knowable is said to be an "obscuration." Whatever sphere of cognitive activity is completely freed from all obscurations to the knowable, just that should be understood to be the domain and sphere of cognitive activity completely purified of the obscurations to the knowable.

The chapter clearly distinguishes between the two classes of Buddhist practitioners and their two respective levels of attainment with respect to knowledge of reality. This distinction is based upon the respective purity of knowledge resulting, on the one hand, from complete freedom from the veil created by the defilements of greed, hatred, and delusion; and on the other hand, from complete freedom from all obscuring veils whatsoever. The first level of purity is obtained by the Hīnayāna practitioners when they have rid themselves of the defilement obscurations. The second, and superior, level of purity is obtained only by the Mahāyāna practitioners, i.e., the Buddhas and the bodhisattvas, who have successfully and completely rid themselves of the final veil obscuring the perfected view of reality. This final veil is referred to as the *jñeyāvaraṇa,* i.e., lit. "the 'covering' or 'obscuration' *(avaraṇa)* to the 'knowable' *(jñeya).*" The two veils are sometimes described as the coarse and subtle obstructions, respectively (1) to liberation and (2) to omniscience. At this point Mahāyāna practitioners are said to possess a knowledge of reality which is freed of the defiling passions, all subjective biases, and the aberrant view of the subject/object, or perceiver/perceived, duality—"completely freed from all obscurations to the knowable." Such ones experience reality directly, as it is *(yathābhūtam)*.

> Again, what is that? It is the domain and the sphere of cognitive activity that belongs to the Buddha-Bhagavans and bodhisattvas who, having penetrated the non-self of dharmas *(dharmanairātmya)*, and having realized, because of that pure understanding, the inexpressible nature *(nirabhilāpya-svabhāvatā)* of all dharmas, know the sameness *(sama)* of the essential nature of verbal designation *(prajñaptivāda)* and the nondiscursive knowable *(nirvikalpajñeya)*. That is the supreme Suchness *(tathatā)*, there being none higher, which is at the extreme limit of the knowable and for which all analyses of the dharmas are accomplished, and which they do not surpass.

Now Asaṅga addresses that knowledge possessed by the Buddhas and bodhisattvas, the focal point of the chapter, describing as he does the central practice and realization of such practitioners. The opening statement of the chapter defined the knowledge of the Buddhas to which the bodhisattva should aspire. Here the text advises such a bodhisattva to take up the "Path of Instruction," which aims at comprehending the "selflessness of all dharmas" *(dharmanairātmya)*. Concomitant with the complete comprehension of *dharma-*

nairātmya is the realization of the inexpressible nature of all dharmas and, hence, the sameness *(samatā)* of essential nature of both verbal designations and those dharmas which are now known directly (i.e. the "nondiscursive dharmas"), freed of all subjective imputations.

Because Asaṅga's approach in this chapter is based upon a careful analysis of names and their relationship to things, the definition of "the supreme Suchness" *(Tathatā)* is given in terms of this analysis. Hence Suchness is made synonymous with Sameness *(Samatā),* where "sameness" refers to the sameness of essential nature of both names and things. It should be remembered that *Tathatā* is a common synonym for *śūnyatā.* By extension, then, both names and the dharmas to which those names are applied have the same essential nature, namely voidness.

When the bodhisattva has fully comprehended *dharma-nairātmya,* he realizes that all dharmas (1) have no independent "self"; (2) have no expressible "self"; and (3) do not, ultimately, allow of imputation. Hence, dharmas do not exist as they are expressed.

But, one should understand, this does not mean that names and dharmas do not exist in any way whatsoever. For Asaṅga both are existent knowables, and may be known directly. Again, to say that the essential nature of names and dharmas (and names too are dharmas) is the same, i.e., voidness, is not to say, for Asaṅga, that they are completely nonexistent. It is precisely the task of the bodhisattva to come to understand *how* each is existent.

> Furthermore, it should be understood that the correctly determined *(vyavasthānataḥ)* characteristic of reality is its 'not-two' *(advaya)* nature, or constitu-

tion *(prabhāvitaṃ)*. The two are said to be "being" *(bhāva)* and "nonbeing" *(abhāva)*.

The Sanskrit passage reads: *tat punaḥ tattva-lakṣaṇaṃ vyavasthānataḥ advayaprabhāvitaṃ veditavyaṃ*. The section is clearly important and is set apart in the Sanskrit from the rest of the text for emphasis. This may be said to be the only passage wherein Asaṅga seems to make an ontological statement with reference to reality. "Correctly determined" renders *vyavasthānataḥ,* which also translates as "established." Here the term seems to refer to the realization of reality "established" by accomplished Mahāyāna practitioners.

The term *advaya* (Tib. *gñis su med pa)* has been purposely given in its literal sense as "not-two" to avoid the connotations engendered by its more common rendering, "nondual." "Nondual" often conjures up the idea of "oneness," which is—in many Yogācāra treatises—inappropriate. For example, in the *Mahāyānasūtrālaṅkāra,* when that text speaks of the *ālayavijñāna* together with the other seven vijñānas, the more correct sense is that the eight vijñānas *function* together, in a totally integrated fashion. That is, they work as *one system.* But it would be incorrect to say that the vijñānas are one, in that context. Likewise, in the context of this chapter, Asaṅga's use of *advaya* is to indicate that the characteristic of reality as determined by the "Accomplished Ones" *transcends* the categories of "being" and "nonbeing"; it is neither completely existent nor completely nonexistent. Rather, in it, both "being" and "nonbeing" function side-by-side, if you will, simultaneously. Such a view is consistent with Asaṅga's central premise here that dharmas are existent, but they are not existent as they are expressed. He is quite careful throughout the chapter not to imply that two distinct aspects of dharmas, i.e., their "noumenal" aspect and their "phenomenal" aspect, are one and the same, but to indicate, rather, that those two aspects are the *same in essence,* since the essential nature *(svabhāva)* of all dharmas is in fact voidness.

Bhāva, rendered here as "being," and *abhāva,* rendered as "nonbeing," may also be translated by "existent" and "nonexistent," respectively. Asaṅga's subsequent listing of examples for *bhāva* indicates that the term refers to specific entities of experience, i.e., "existent things"; and hence not to the more general, more abstract rendering "existence" in this context.

> With regard to those two, "being" is whatever is determined to have essential nature solely by virtue of verbal designation *(prajñaptivāda svabhāva),* and as such is clung to by the worldly for a long time. For ordinary beings, this [notion of "being"] is the root of all discursive thought *(vikalpa)* and proliferation *(prapañca),* whether "form," "feeling," "ideation," "motivation" or "perception"; "eye," "ear," "nose," "tongue," "body," or "mind"; "earth," "water," "fire," or "wind"; "form," "sound," "smell," "taste," or "contact"; "skillful" "unskillful," or "indeterminate" acts; "birth" or "passing away" or "dependent arising"; "past," "future," or "present"; "compounded" or "uncompounded"; "This is a world, and beyond is a world," "There are both the sun and moon," and whatever is "seen," "heard," "believed," or "perceived"; what is "attained or striven for," what is "adumbrated" or "thought with signs" by the mind; even up to "Nirvāṇa." Every-

> thing in this category has a nature established by verbal designation only. This is said [by ordinary beings] to be "being."

As mentioned earlier, because ordinary beings use language in a careless—though habitual and conditioned—way, such "worldly ones" continually fall into the error of assuming that names accurately characterize the essential nature of the things named. Here also Asaṅga implies that, for ordinary beings, there is the further assumption that *whatever can be named, exists*—for example, a 'person' (and vice-versa: if a thing exists, it can be named).

In his exegesis of this chapter, at folio 22b.4, Asaṅga, again using the five aggregates, gives an example to illustrate this first mistaken view: "one should understand that immature [Tib. *byis pa rnam pa,* Skt. *bālaḥ,* lit. "children"] beings cling to expressible given things as being, or having, the nature of their names and their expressions. . . . That being the case, to the question "What is the nature of that given thing?" an immature one would answer "Its nature is form" but would not answer, "Its *name* is 'form'." And he would answer that its nature is feeling, ideation, motivation, or perception; and would not answer that " 'perception' is [but] its name." And so for all the other [aggregates], respectively."

As is typical for works of this kind, Asaṅga begins his enumeration of examples of "being" by listing the five *skandhas,* or "aggregates," said to comprise and delimit a 'being' as a 'person', or 'individual' namely: form *(rūpa),* feeling *(vedanā),* ideation *(saṃjñā),* motivation *(saṃskāra),* and perception *(vijñāna)*. Here the aggregate, "form," is intended to cover the material or physical aspect of the world and, traditionally, comprises the four elements (best rendered, solidity, fluidity, heat, and motion), the five material sense-organs, and their corresponding objects in the external world. Consequently, "form" serves as a catch-all term, in Buddhist contexts in general and in Asaṅga's text in particular, for indicating any ostensible object.

Vikalpa (rnam pa rtog pa) means "discursive thought" of any sort, i.e., thought that is generally unbridled or undisciplined. It moves rapidly and uncontrollably, generating fictions of the imagination. Though it is usually treated as having a negative connotation (especially in meditative contexts, and in the present context of this chapter), the term sometimes also bears a positive meaning, viz., *samyakvikalpa* in Buddhist logic, as in Dharmakīrti's works and in Āryasūra's *Paramītasamāsa.* In these contexts, *samyakvikalpa* is any thought that is virtuous and leads one on the Path of Dharma. Also, though *vikalpa* in the present context of the chapter bears a negative connotation, we have Asaṅga's exegesis in which it appears as one of the "Five Dharmas" offering a positive analysis of successive stages to enlightenment, and hence is treated as one of the constituents of progress on the Buddhist Path.

Prapañca (spros pa), or "proliferation," on the other hand, is always viewed negatively. It is that use of thought which immediately distorts reality, through either exaggeration *(samāropa)* or underestimation *(apavada).* The passage tells us that the view that there is existence purely by virtue of designations is the root *(mūla; rtsa ba)* of all errant thought and distorting proliferations.

With regard to those two, "nonbeing" is the absence of the base of the verbal designation "form," and so on up to "Nirvāṇa," its absence or noncharacterizableness; when the basis of verbal designation, with recourse to which verbal designation operates, is insubstantial, nonascertainable, nonexistent, or non-present in any way whatsoever. This is said to be "nonbeing."

The terms used here for "base" and "basis" are *aśraya* and *āśritya,* respectively. (Later in the chapter, *adhiṣṭhāna* and *saṃniśrayam* will be used as synonyms for these terms.) As just before, Asaṅga is continuing his description of ordinary beings' ideas regarding the "two extremes" of "being" and "nonbeing." Here we are told that ordinary beings consider that whatever does not serve, or cannot be *ascertained* or determined to serve, as a base (referent) onto which one can attach a label does not "exist." Ordinary beings cannot fathom the idea that there can exist a thing which cannot be given a name. Hence, what is not expressible is, for them, nonexistent also. Again, Asaṅga's own commentary is helpful in further clarifying the passage. The section in the exegesis is devoted specifically to illuminating the mutual dependence and mutual arising of names and things, but will nevertheless be quoted here in full:

[23b.5] How should one understand that there is bondage by virtue of expressions for signs? He [the Buddha] said: "It should be understood by reasoning and by scripture. What is the reasoning? . . . If there is no expression, then one cannot take pleasure in a given thing; but if there is accompanying expression, then one takes pleasure in it. This is one reason.

Moreover, the one is the birthplace of the other; that is, the thought [Tib. *dmigs-pa*] which gives rise to expression is dependent upon a given thing; and the thought which gives rise to a given thing is dependent upon an expression. Accordingly, for example, worldly beings may imagine given things by means of name and expression; *but if given things are not present, then they are unable to imagine them.* Since that is the case, then the thought which gives rise to name and expression is dependent upon the given thing. . . .

Whenever a definitive statement is made concerning truth or falsity in Mahāyāna texts, in general the Buddha himself is considered to have spoken it—whether or not such statements are direct quotations from scriptural sources. Asaṅga's exegesis of the chapter is replete with such passages, all prefaced by *āha* (Tib. *smras pa),* literally "he said," where "he" clearly refers to the Buddha.

The point of this passage, put simply, is that for ordinary beings, things which are not present, and hence cannot be named, are considered to be nonexistent. Of course, this is a mistaken view according to Asaṅga's position, since we have been told previously that dharmas do exist even though their essential nature is inexpressible *(nirabhilāpya)* and beyond the reach of designation.

For my "imagine" the Tibetan uses *rab tu rtog pa* and *yoṅs su rtog pa.* Alternate renderings in this context are "think about," "consider," or "entertain in the mind."

Moreover, the given thing, comprised of dharma characteristics, that is completely freed from both "being" and "nonbeing"—i.e., from the "being" and "nonbeing" described above—is "not-two." Now, what is not-two, just that is said to be the incomparable Middle Path *(madhyamā pratipad)* which avoids the two extremes; and concerning *that* reality *(tattve)* the knowledge *(jñānam)* of all the Buddha-

Bhagavans should be understood to be exceedingly pure. Further, it should be understood that that knowledge for the bodhisattvas constitutes the Path of Instruction *(śikṣā-mārga)*.

By way of summarizing the foregoing discussion in the chapter, Asaṅga now clearly sets forth the Middle Path mode of viewing which is consistent with the highest type of knowledge of reality, possessed by all the Buddhas. Such cognition views an existent given thing directly, freed from the subjective constructs of "being" and "nonbeing," and hence, without superimposing any labels or assignations whatsoever unto that existent base. The Buddhas, being freed of the "veils" *(avaraṇas)* of defiling passions and of subjective biases, have accomplished this mode of cognizing all dharmas. Asaṅga now begins to describe the practices that the bodhisattvas, aspiring after such knowledge, should take up.

Śikṣā-mārga (Tib. *slob pa'i lam)* refers, in Buddhist tradition, to the three higher trainings *(adhiśikṣas)*, viz. in (1) conduct *(śīla)*, (2) meditative concentration *(samādhi)*, and (3) insight *(prajñā)*. In the passage just given above, Asaṅga has identified the last of these, i.e., *prajñā,* with the insight which views the not-two reality of the given thing perceived. In the passage that follows, he tells us that the cultivation of this insight is the "great means" *(mahān upāya;* Tib. *thabs chen po)* for the bodhisattva seeking superior knowledge of reality.

That insight *(prajñā)* is the bodhisattva's great means *(mahān upāya)* for reaching the Incomparable Perfect Enlightenment. And why? Because of the bodhisattva's firm conviction in voidness *(śūnyatādhimokṣa)*, practicing in these and those births and circling in saṃsāra for the sake of thoroughly ripening *(paripākāya)* the Buddhadharmas for himself and other sentient beings, he comes to know saṃsāra as it really is *(yathābhūtam)*. And moreover, he does not weary his mind with the aspects *(ākārā)* of impermanence and so forth *(anityādibhir)* which pertain to that saṃsāra. Should he not experience the true nature of saṃsāra, he would be unable, owing to all the defilements—of lust, hatred, delusion, and so forth—to render his mind equable; and not being equable, his defiled mind, circling in saṃsāra, would mature neither the Buddhadharmas nor the sentient beings.

Śūnyatādhimokṣa (Tib. *stoṅ pa ñid la mos pa*): Edgerton, in his *Buddhist Hybrid Sanskrit Dictionary*, defines *adhimokṣa* as "zealous devotion," and the Tibetan term *mos pa* refers to "one who is addicted" to any thing. But voidness itself is not a thing, to which one can or should become attached. As mentioned in the Introduction, both Nāgārjuna and Asaṅga wished to correct such a mistaken view. The rendering "firm conviction in voidness" is phrased thus to avoid this mistaken connotation.

The term *paripākāya* (Tib. *yoṅs su smin par bya ba)* is connected with "maturing" ordinary beings, often referred to as *bālas* (Tib. *byis pa)*, literally "children"—those whose knowledge, particularly of Buddhist doctrine, is undeveloped. Sarat Candra Das defines the *bāla* as "one who is unskilled in the knowledge of karma"; but it is used in much broader senses, encompassing all the Buddhist doctrine.

Contrasted, of course, with such beings is the bodhisattva, who has as his chief duty bringing the sentient beings to "maturity."

The *ākāras* or "aspects" of saṃsāra are traditionally taught in association with the Four Noble Truths. They were twelve in the earliest teaching, and later were crystallized into a set of sixteen, beginning with *anitya* (impermanence), *duḥkha* (suffering), and *anātman* (non-self).

In the next few passages Asaṅga indicates that the bodhisattva seeking the superior knowledge of reality should not seek the Nirvāṇa of the śrāvakas and pratyekabuddhas. Nor should he disparage that goal, nor be frightened by it. Rather, he should remain equable and firmly rooted in his conviction in voidness.

> Again, if he should weary his mind with the aspects of saṃsāra, impermanence, and so forth, being thus [wearied] that bodhisattva would very quickly enter Parinirvāṇa. But the bodhisattva thus entering very quickly into Parinirvāṇa would mature neither the Buddhadharmas nor the sentient beings. Again, how would he become awakened to the Incomparable Perfect Enlightenment?
>
> On account of his firm conviction in voidness, that bodhisattva, continuously applying himself, is neither frightened by Nirvāṇa nor does he strive toward Nirvāṇa. If that bodhisattva should be frightened by Nirvāṇa, he would not store up his equipment for Nirvāṇa hereafter; but rather, not seeing the benefits which lie in Nirvāṇa, owing to fear of it, that bodhisattva would give up the faith and conviction which sees the excellent qualities in that.

On the other hand, if that bodhisattva should frequently fix [his or her mind] zealously on Parinirvāṇa, he would speedily enter Parinirvāṇa. But as a result of quickly entering Parinirvāṇa, he would mature neither the Buddhadharmas nor the sentient beings.

In summary, whoever does not thoroughly experience saṃsāra as it really is circles in saṃsāra with a defiled mind. And whoever is wearied in mind by saṃsāra quickly enters Nirvāṇa. Whoever possesses a mind of fear with respect to Nirvāṇa does not store up equipment for it. And whoever fixes [his or her mind] zealously on Nirvāṇa quickly enters Parinirvāṇa. But it should be understood that these are not the bodhisattva's means for attaining Incomparable Perfect Enlightenment.

Again, whoever thoroughly experiences saṃsāra as it really is circles in saṃsāra with an undefiled mind. And whoever has a mind which is unwearied by the aspects of impermanence and so forth of saṃsāra, that one does not quickly enter Nirvāṇa. And whoever has a mind which is unfrightened by Nirvāṇa stores up equipment for it, and though seeing the good qualities and benefits in Nirvāṇa, still does not exceedingly long for it, and so does not quickly enter Nirvāṇa. This is the bodhisattva's great means for attaining the Incomparable Perfect Enlightenment. And this means is well grounded in that firm conviction in supreme voidness. Therefore for the bodhisattva who has well taken hold of the Path of Instruction, cultivating conviction in supreme voidness is said to be the "Great Means" for reaching the knowledge of the Tathāgata.

Now you should know that that bodhisattva, because of his long-time engagement with the knowledge of dharma-selflessness, having understood the inexpressibility of all dharmas as they really are, does not at all imagine *(kalpayati)* any dharma; otherwise he would not [truly] grasp "given thing only" as precisely "Suchness only." It does not occur to him, "This is the given thing only, and this other, the Suchness only." In clear understanding the bodhisattva courses, and coursing in this supreme understanding with insight into Suchness, he sees all dharmas as they really are, i.e., as being absolutely the same. And seeing everywhere sameness, his mind likewise, he attains to supreme equanimity.

The bodhisattva attains to supreme equanimity *(paramāṃ upekṣāṃ)* as a result of his/her cultivation of and engagement with the knowledge of dharma-selflessness. Concomitant with this knowledge is the realization of the inexpressible nature of all the dharmas and of the sameness of their essential nature. The passage is clear in identifying Suchness *(tathatā)* with sameness of essential nature *(samatā)*. Because of this realization of sameness, the bodhisattva does not *imagine* any dharma. That is, because he no longer possesses discursive thought *(vikalpa)* or constructive imagination *(kalpanā)*—which superimposes constructs, judgments, designations, and distinctions—he perceives no distinctions when viewing dharmas; but rather, when seeing dharmas, he sees Suchness.

> Taking recourse in that equanimity, while greatly applying himself toward skill in all the sciences, that bodhisattva does not turn away from his goal because of fatigue, or because of any suffering. Unwearied in body and unwearied in mind, he quickly achieves skillfulness in those [sciences], and he reaches the stage of attaining the great power of mindfulness. He is not puffed up by virtue of his skill, nor does he have a teacher's closed-fistedness toward others. Not only does his mind not shrink from any skills, but also, with enthusiasm, he proceeds without hindrance.

"Skill in all the sciences" refers to the bodhisattva's tireless devotion to mastering all the *vidyasthānas* (Tib. *rig pa'i gnas),* which, according to Buddhist tradition, are five in number: (1) Buddhist philosophy, (2) logic, (3) grammar, (4) medicine, and (5) the technical arts and crafts. With these skills, the bodhisattva is better able to convert and otherwise benefit beings.

"Great power of mindfulness" = *mahāsmṛtibala;* Tib. *dran-pa'i stob-pa bskyed-pa chen-po.* Dayal, in his *Bodhisattva Doctrine,* p. 82, says that "*Smṛti* is the *sine qua non* or moral progress for a bodhisattva." It is an essential part of a bodhisattva's equipment *(sambhara);* and its possession confers great power *(bala)* on him/her. For a more thorough analysis of this term, see Dayal, pp. 82 ff.

"Closed-fistedness of a teacher" renders the Sanskrit *ācāryamuṣṭiṃ* (Tib. *slob-dpon gyi dpe-mkhyud).* Edgerton *(Buddhist Hybrid Sanskrit Dictionary,* p. 89) defines this term as "close fistedness of a teacher, keeping things (particularly instruction) back from pupils." Bodhisattvas are made neither proud nor arrogant by their attainments; nor are they stingy with those skills, knowledge, or belongings which they possess.

Practicing with steadfast mental armor *(dṛḍha-saṃnāha):*

to the extent that circling in saṃsāra he experiences diverse sufferings *(duḥkha-viśeṣam),* to that extent he generates enthusiasm toward Incomparable Perfect Enlightenment;

to the extent that he experiences diverse bodies *(samucchraya-viśeṣam),* to that extent he lacks pride toward any sentient being;

to the extent that he experiences diverse acquaintances [?] *(jñāna-viśeṣam),* to that extent when associated with others seeking brawls and disputes, who are garrulous, have great and lesser defilements, and who practice unbridled and mistaken ways, as he experiences those ones, even to greater measure his mind stays in equanimity;

and to the extent that he grows in virtue *(guṇas),* to that extent his goodness *(kalyāṇa)* is unabated.

He does not seek to know from others nor does he seek gain or reverence [for himself]. These and numerous other benefits *(anuśaṃsā)* of the same category, i.e., the Wings of Enlightenment dharmas and all things consistent with Enlightenment, accrue for the bodhisattva who has that knowledge as his excellent basis. Therefore, whoever sets out to attain Enlightenment, whoever will attain it, and those who do attain it, all these have as their basis that very same knowledge—not another knowledge, whether superior or inferior.

The "Wings of Enlightenment" dharmas (Skt. *bodhipakṣya;* Tib. *byaṅ chub kyi phyogs)* refers to a traditional Buddhist formula comprised of thirty-seven factors, or practices, held to be conducive to enlightenment. These factors include the four *smṛty-upasthānāni,* or mindfulness meditations; four *samyak prahāṇāni,* right efforts; four *ṛddhi-pādāh,* or bases of magical efficiency; the five *īndriyāṇi,* or controlling moral and spiritual values; five *balāni,* strengths or powers; seven *bodhy-aṅgāni,* i.e., constituents of enlightenment; and the Noble Eightfold Way, equaling thirty-seven. For a fuller treatment of the *bodhipakṣya* doctrine, see Dayal, *Bodhisattva Doctrine,* pp. 80–164.

Having thus entered upon the practical application of the method without proliferation, the bodhisattva has many benefits: he rightly engages in thoroughly ripening the Buddhadharmas for himself, and for others, in thoroughly ripening the Dharma of the Three Vehicles. Moreover, thus rightly engaged, he is without craving for possessions or even for his own body.

The "Three Vehicles" *(yānatraya; theg pa gsum)* are (1) the Śrāvaka Vehicle, (2) the Pratyekabuddha Vehicle, and (3) the Bodhisattva Vehicle.

He trains *(śikṣate)* himself in noncraving so that he is able to give to sentient beings his possessions and even his own body. For the sake of sentient beings alone is he restrained, and well restrained, in body and speech. He trains himself in restraint so that he naturally takes no pleasure in sin, and so that he becomes wholesome and good by nature. He is forbearing toward all injury and wrongdoing on the part of others. He trains himself in forbearance so that he has little anger and so that he does no injury to others.

The verb *śikṣate* (Tib. *slob-pa),* though a common term, is interesting here. It has the connotations of both "to teach" and "to learn." The bodhisattva learns by doing and so teaches him/herself. The dual sense of the term has been kept by the rendering "trains."

He becomes skillful and expert in all the sciences in order to dispell the doubts *(vicikitsā)* of sentient beings and to manage to assist them, and for himself, to embrace the cause of omniscience *(sarvajñānatā).* His mind abides within, equipoised. And he trains himself in the fixing of his mind, so as to completely purify the Four Sublime Abodes *(caturbrāhmavihāra),* and to sport in the Five Supernormal Faculties *(pañcābhijñā)* in order to perform his duty toward all sentient beings, and in order to clear away the fatigue that arose from his exertions to become expert. And he becomes wise, knowing the Supreme Reality *(paramatattvajñā).* He trains himself to know the Supreme Reality, so that in the future he will himself, in the Great Vehicle, enter Parinirvāṇa.

Vicikitsa (Tib. *the tshom),* or doubt, is the sixth of the ten kleśas, defiling passions, in the Pāli enumeration and the last of the Mahāyāna listing of six kleśas. It is considered to be one of the major hindrances to spiritual progress. Dispelling the doubts of sentient beings, especially with regard to the Dharma, is one of the primary offerings made by the bodhisattva as he/she seeks the welfare of all beings.

The "Four Sublime Abodes" *(catur-brāhma-vihāras; tshans pa'i gnas bźi)* are four meditations which in the Buddhist tradition are called *brāhma-vihāras,* "brāhma" denoting here not the Hindu god but the state or level of "noble accomplishment" that the bodhisattva achieves by practicing these. The same four are also known as the *apramāṇas,* the "infinitudes," the "measureless" or "boundless" meditations. Edward Conze, in *Buddhist Thought in India,* p. 80, suggests that the four seem to have belonged to the Indian religious traditions as a whole, since they are also found, listed in the same order, in Patañjali's *Yoga-sūtras.*

The four *brāhma-vihāras* consist of cultivating, through prescribed meditative techniques, four particular feelings: (1) *maitri,* love, or friendliness; (2) *karuṇa,* compassion; (3) *mudita,* sympathetic joy; and (4) *upekṣa,* or equanimity. A good description of the four sets within the meditative tradition is given by Mahāthera in his *Buddhist Meditation.*

The Venerable Tri-chang Rinpoche, current Head Tutor to the 14th Dalai Lama, has described these practices. He says that, first and foremost, it is important to develop *upekṣa,* for without it, the other three vihāras cannot be successfully accomplished. Moreover, when seeking to develop *maitri, karuṇa,* and *mudita,* it is important to begin with a genuine feeling of each. The practice is not aimed at expanding or making "unlimited" these emotions themselves, for if this were the case, then one would not in fact be working with genuine feeling. That is, true friendliness does not change. Rather, the practice of the vihāras is performed so that the *number of sentient beings* one is able to include within those emotions or address them to is made "unlimited." The Rinpoche's description of these practices seems the most accurate accounting and is consistent with the order given by Asaṅga in the passage above, viz., the bodhisattva, being first "equipoised," fixes his mind on the cultivation of the brāhma-vihāras.

Dayal, *Bodhisattva Doctrine,* p. 226, tells us that by the time of the *Prajñāpāramitā* literature, the term *apramāṇa* supersedes the use of *vihāra;* and that this was probably due to later, specific, use of *vihāra* "to denote the different stages of a bodhisattva's spiritual career."

Further, we are told, the bodhisattva accomplishes the "five supernormal faculties" (Skt. *pañcābhijñā; mṅon par śes pa lṅa).* The *abhijñās,* or "supernormal faculties," are listed here as being five, but are also enumerated as six in, for example, the *Mahāyānasūtrālaṅkāra.* Dayal (in *The Bodhisattva Doctrine,* p. 107) cites the *Mahāvyutpatti* for his listing of the six *abhijñās,* as follows: (1) *divyaṃ cakṣuh,* i.e., divine seeing; (2) *divyaṃ śrotram,* divine hearing; (3) *parasya ceta-paryāya-jñānam,* knowing the makeup of others' thoughts; (4) *pūrva-nivas-anusmṛti-jñānam,* memory of past lives; (5) *ṛddhi-vidhi-jñānam,* knowing magical powers; and (6) *āsrava-kṣaya-jñānam,* knowing the destruction of the outflows.

The *Daśabhūmikasūtra* omits the sixth *abhijñā,* as does Asaṅga here. Presumably, Asaṅga does so because he includes the "destruction of the outflows" *(āsrava-kṣaya)* earlier in the chapter, among the attainments accomplished by the śrāvakas and pratyekabuddhas, and views this accomplishment as being consistent with the destruction of the veil of defiling passions.

The *abhijñās* are sometimes treated as falling into two main divisions, viz., mundane *(lokiya)* and supramundane *(lokottara)*. According to this analysis, those accomplishments of the first division are the result of practicing *śamatha,* or meditation aimed at "calming"; and those of the second category are attained through *vipaśyana,* or meditation aimed at "insight." Van Zeyst, in the *Encyclopaedia of Buddhism,* p. 98, says that the five abhijñās fall into the first category, while the sixth—and sometimes even a seventh—member falls into the latter category. Moreover, of the fivefold listing, four are said to pertain to knowledge (i.e., divine hearing, knowing the makeup of others' thoughts, magical powers, and memory of former lives), while the fifth, "divine seeing," has to do solely with vision and pertains to the ability of Buddhas and bodhisattvas to see the various "passings away and rebirths of beings."

"In the future he will himself, in the Great Vehicle, enter Parinirvāṇa," *mahāyāne c'āyatyām ātmanaḥ parinirvāṇāya,* is interesting because of the rather concrete way in which Asaṅga uses the locative case of the term *mahāyāna,* i.e., as literally "*in* the great vehicle."

You should know that the bodhisattva thus rightly engaged carefully attends all virtuous beings with worship and reverence. And all unvirtuous being he carefully attends with a mind of sympathy and a mind of supreme compassion.

And insofar as he can and has the strength he is engaged in dispersing their faults. He carefully attends all harmful beings with a mind of love. And insofar as he can and has the strength, being himself without trickery *(aśaṭha)* and without deceit *(amāyāvī)*, he works for their benefit and happiness, to eliminate the hostile consciousness of those who do evil because of their faults *(doṣa)* of expectation and practice. Unto helpful beings, after showing gratitude, he carefully attends them in return with more than equal helpfulness. And he fulfills their pious aspirations as much as he is able and as much as is his strength. Even when he is unable, not having been asked, he displays respectful endeavor toward these and those duties to be done. Never once does he reject duty. How should the notion occur to him, "I, being incapable, do not wish to do this"? This, and other actions of the same category, should be understood as the right procedure for the bodhisattva who, having taken up the way of nonproliferation, is well based in knowledge of Supreme Reality.

"Even when he is unable. . . . ": the various Sanskrit and Tibetan editions disagree in their renderings of this passage. Wogihara's Sanskrit version reads as follows: *apratibalo'pi ca yācitaḥ san teṣu teṣu kṛtya-karaṇiyeṣv ādāraṃ-vyāyāmam upadarśayati na sakṛd eva nirākaroti.* Dutt's edition agrees with Wogihara's except for its reading *ādaraṃ*, "respectful," as opposed to *ādāraṃ* (?). Wogihara's text, however, does give a note, p. 43, suggesting the alternate rendering.

The Tibetan version clearly reads *gus par,* i.e., *ādaraṃ,* but also differs from both Wogihara's and Dutt's versions by reading *ma bcol bar,* i.e., *na yācitah,* (lit.) "when *not* being solicited" rather than *ca yācitah,* "and being solicited."

The translation given here follows the Tibetan rendering of the passage. Since all the editions agree in their reading that it would not occur to the bodhisattva to reject action on the grounds that he/she is incapable of performing a duty, it clearly seems more appropriate to the context that he/she is "unable" to act only in cases where there has been no direct petition or appointment to perform a given service—i.e., where there has been no specific request. Such behavior demonstrates the bodhisattva's restraint and attention to effective, selfless service rather than his/her inability.

[II]

Now by what philosophical reasoning is the inexpressible character *(nirabhilāpya-svabhāvatā)* of all dharmas to be understood? As follows: Whatever is a designation for the individual characteristics of the dharmas, for example, "form" or "feeling" or the other personality aggregrates, or, as before explained, even up to "Nirvāṇa," that should be understood to be only a designation *(prajñapti-mātram).* It is neither the essential nature *(svabhāva)* of that dharma, nor is it wholly other than that. That [essential nature] is neither the sphere of speech nor the object of speech; nor is it altogether different from these. That being the case, the essential nature of dharmas is not found in the way in which it

> is expressed; but further, neither is absolutely nothing found. Again, the essential nature is absent *(avidyamāna)* and yet not absolutely absent. One might ask: "How is it found?" It is found by avoiding grasping both the view which affirms the existence of what is nonexistent and the view which denies existence altogether. Moreover, one should understand that only the sphere of cognitive activity which is completely freed of discursive thought is the domain of knowledge of the supreme essential nature *(paramārthikaḥ svabhāvaḥ)* of all dharmas.

With this passage, Asaṅga begins the explication of the philosophical reasoning *(yukti)* by which the bodhisattva comes to realize the inexpressible essential nature of all dharmas. Having completed the description of the *practices* that the bodhisattva should cultivate, Asaṅga now addresses the central topic of the chapter. Here the key term, *prajñapti-mātra*, "just" or "only a designation," is introduced, and the philosophical approach adopted in the chapter—i.e., the analysis of the relationship between designations and the essential nature of dharmas—is prominently posed. In the passages that follow, Asaṅga will present a careful analysis of the nature of designations and of their relationship both to individual dharmas (here, all referents of names) and to essential nature in general.

The Sanskrit of this passage is especially interesting largely for the ambiguity introduced by its use of *tad*, "that," or "it." The passage reads:

prajñapti-mātram eva tad veditavyaṃ.
na svabhāvo nāpi ca tad-vinirmuktas

tad anyo vāg-gocaro vāg-viṣayaḥ.
evaṃ sati na svabhāvo dharmāṇāṃ
tathā vidyate.

Here "that" may be seen as applying equally and simultaneously to "designation" and to "essential nature," such that the passage may be rendered (first *tad),* "designations are not equivalent to the essential nature of dharmas," and (second *tad)* "essential nature is not the sphere of speech nor the object of speech." The ambiguity may well be intentional here, emphasizing—from both directions—the absence of essential nature in/through designations.

The passage concludes with a clear description of the Middle Path mode of viewing essential nature and with the reiteration that such cognition is possible only when discursive thought has been completely silenced. There follows, in the next few passages, a brief debate-style analysis wherein Asaṅga gives critiques of the assumptions, first, that names impart essential nature to the things named; and second, that the things themselves dictate what names should be applied to them.

> Again, if with regard to any dharma or any given thing it is assumed that it becomes just like its expression, then those dharmas and that given thing would be that expression itself. But if that were the case, then for a single dharma and a single given thing there would be very many kinds of essential nature. And why? It is like this: to a single dharma and to a single given thing, various men will attach many different designations by virtue of numerous expressions of various kinds. That dharma and that

> given thing ought to have identity with, be made up of, and have the essential nature of some one verbal designation, but not of the other remaining verbal designations. But there being no fixed determination, which of the very many kinds of verbal designation would hold as the correct one? Therefore, the use of any and all verbal designations, however complete or incomplete, for any and all given things does *not* mean that the latter are identical to, made up of, or receive essential nature through those verbal designations.

The assumption that a thing "matches" its designation raises numerous problems. One implies by such an assumption that a particular given thing is identical with, made up of, and has the essential nature of *the* name applied to it. But, Asaṅga argues, this cannot be so, since for any one particular thing, many different names are applied—by different beings and under different circumstances. The varied designations, it should be clear, are the results not only of different languages but also of differing psychological situations, emotional responses, and their consequent perceptions. For example, I am reminded of the common Yogācāra illustration cited by Edward Conze under his discussion of "The Yogācārins" in *Buddhist Thought in India.* The illustration points out that beings at different stages of rebirth perceive things differently: "One and the same object, say a river, leads to totally different ideas on the part of hungry ghosts, animals, men and gods. . . . The hungry ghosts, by way of retribution of their past deeds, see nothing but pus, urine and excrement; fishes find there a home; men see fresh and pure water which can be used for washing and drinking; the gods of the station of infinite space see only space" (p. 256). Such differing perceptions, of course, generate the use of different designations for the same given thing. Since there is no "fixed determination" for choosing which of the various names is *the* correct one—i.e., *the* one which accurately characterizes the essential nature of that given thing—the bodhisattva should understand that *the essential nature of things is neither found in, nor imparted by, the names applied to those things.*

> Now, to view it in another way, suppose the dharmas themselves, of form and so forth, as previously expounded, should become the essential nature of their verbal designations. If this were the case, then, first there would be just the given thing alone, i.e., completely disassociated from names, and only afterward would there be the desire to attach to that given thing a verbal designation. But this would mean that before a verbal designation was attached, at the time just prior to attaching the designation, that very dharma and that very given thing would be without essential nature. But if there were no essential nature, there would be no given thing at all; and hence, a designation would not be called for. And since no verbal designation would be attached, the essential nature of the dharma and of the given thing could not be proved.

This second hypothesis supposes that things "take on" or come to possess essential nature once they are named. Asaṅga counters this assumption directly; if no prior existent essential nature is assumed, then no prior thing is present, and no object is available to serve as a base onto which to attach a name. A name is applied to some thing. If there is no thing present, then there is no occasion even to pursue the question of whether or not its name accurately characterizes its essential nature. Hence, whatever be the essential nature possessed by things, that essential nature cannot be said to be verbally established, i.e., to have begun to exist as a result of the naming process.

> Again, suppose that just prior to the attaching of a verbal designation, that dharma and that given thing should be identical with the designation. This being the case, even without the verbal designation "form," the idea of form would occur whenever there was a dharma with the name "form," and whenever there was a given thing with the name "form." But such does not occur.
>
> Now, through employing reasoning like this, one should understand that the essential nature of all dharmas is inexpressible, i.e., completely beyond the reach of expression. And one should understand that just as with regard to form, so with feelings, etc., as previously expounded, even up to Nirvāṇa itself.

Whereas the first two assumptions addressed the issue of names and things from the side of names and suggested that designations truly defined or imparted essential nature to things, the above passage speaks from the side of the things themselves and considers the proposition that the essential nature of things already is such that it defines and dictates what names should properly be applied to them. But, were it true that things themselves dictated their correct names, then there should be complete and universal agreement about what each thing is called. Moreover, such universal agreement should exist despite the various language, perceptual, and psychological responses mentioned before. But clearly this is not the case. Through reasoning such as this, one should understand that the essential nature of all dharmas is "beyond the reach of expression." And yet, Asaṅga assures us, the essential nature of dharmas does exist. He now begins, in a thoroughgoing fashion, to expound how knowledge of this inexpressible essential nature may be obtained.

> It should be understood that these two views have fallen away from our Dharma-Vinaya: (1) that one which clings to affirming *(samāropata)* the existence of what are nonexistent individual characteristics, having essential nature only through verbal designations for a given thing, form, etc., or for the dharmas form and so forth; and also (2) that one which, with respect to a given thing *(vastu)*, denies *(apavadamāno)* the foundation for the sign of verbal designation, and the basis for the sign of verbal designation, which exists in an ultimate sense *(paramārthasadbhūtaṃ)* owing to its inexpressible essence *(nirabhilāpyātmakatayā)*, saying "absolutely everything is nonexistent."

Asaṅga's statement of these two errant views serves as the peak point of his explication of reality as it should properly be understood. It represents Asaṅga's own formulation of the true Middle Path *(madhyamā pratipad),* the Path that avoids the two erroneous extremes—of existence and nonexistence, of eternalism and nihilism—and the Path that accomplishes the clear explication and vindication of the doctrine of śūnyatā.

The terms, *samāropa* (Tib. *sgro 'dogs pa)* and *apavada (skur pa 'debs),* meaning "affirmation" and "denial," respectively, form a technical pair representing the two extremes. *Samāropa* indicates the extreme of exaggeration, or attributing too much reality to the thing in question; while *apavada* indicates the extreme of underestimation, or attributing too little reality to it. The mean between these two errant views is the Middle Path, which reveals the characteristic of śūnyatā as neither existent nor nonexistent, but rather a mean transcendent to both of those. O'Brien ("A Chapter on Reality," p. 294, note 52) gives an interesting citation from the *Fo-hsing-lun* (T. 31, 795) which centers on the concept of voidness, or emptiness, in its description of the Middle Path: "If one imagines emptiness as existing, this is called exaggeration; if one imagines emptiness as not existing this is called minimizing (i.e., *apavada).*"

Again, Asaṅga's statement is more complex than the traditional statement of the Middle Path (for example, as stated by Nāgārjuna) because it is in keeping with Asaṅga's position that the illusory or the unreal nature (i.e., the *parikalpita)* as well as the relative nature (the *paratantra)* must nevertheless be grounded in the real. That is, his formulation allows for an existent, though inexpressible, substratum of reality (which makes cognition, however distorted, and naming possible at all).

The second part of Asaṅga's formulation may be viewed as being directed particularly at those "outsiders" (i.e., adherents of any of the orthodox Hindu schools) as well as "insiders" (here, followers of the Mādhyamika) who have wrongly conceived śūnyatā to be rank nihilism. To "imagine emptiness as not existing" is a serious mistake which according to Asaṅga has "fallen away" from what properly constitutes true Buddhist doctrine.

For Asaṅga's system, the name or designation is purely of imaginary nature *(parikalpita)*. His exegesis states (27b.3): "How should one thoroughly know imaginary nature? He said: One should thoroughly know that imaginary nature as being merely name, to wit, merely imagination." The *vastu,* or given thing, however, does exist—as *paratantra,* or relative nature. That is, since it is compounded, it exists, though impermanently and hence not in an absolute sense. Again, the exegesis states (27b.7): "How should one thoroughly know dependency nature? He said: One should thoroughly know that it includes all constructed things [*bya ba 'dus byas,* lit. "created through compounding"]." By "compounded" is meant produced through conditions, or "come together owing to causes and conditions." An alternate name for *vastu* in this sense is "conditioned thing." Any conditioned phenomenon is dependent (upon causes and conditions) and, owing to this dependence, is impermanent. Hence the ultimate state or mode of reality is often referred to as "the Unconditioned."

Hence while the denial of the *vastu* (in the passage synonymous with *nimitta* = "sign," or "the thing upon which speech is based"), is permissible—if one understands the *proper sense* of the denial—it is a grave error to deny the existence of the inexpressible [ultimate] *foundation (adhiṣṭhānaṃ)* of that *vastu.* For, according to Asaṅga, that inexpressible foundation does exist in an ultimate sense. It is the true, *pariniṣpanna,* reality.

The faults which result from affirming the existence of what is nonexistent have been examined, laid out, clarified, and illumined immediately above. Because of these faults which arise from affirming the existence of nonexistents with respect to the given thing of form, etc., one should understand that view as having fallen away from our Dharma-Vinaya.

Ordinary beings do this all the time whenever they apply names to things and believe—without ever pondering the validity of their belief—that things exist just as they are expressed. By so carelessly engaging in language and judgment games, we continually superimpose unto things attributes and characteristics which are nonexistent in fact. Hence we exaggerate the true state of affairs.

Likewise, denying the bare given thing *(vastu-mātram)*, which is a universal denial *(sarvavaināśika)*, has fallen away from our Dharma-Vinaya. I say, then: "Neither reality nor designation is known when the bare given thing, of form and so forth, is denied. Both these views are incorrect."

The compound term, *vastu-mātram,* has been translated as "bare given thing" in an attempt to render the special sense, I think intended here, of a base or thing completely free of attributes or imputations. It may also here be rendered simply as "the given thing itself" (i.e. apart from subjective impositions). Asaṅga's point is that according to the Middle

Path mode of viewing, it is in error to affirm the existence of what is in fact nonexistent and it is in error to deny existence altogether. Here the emphasis is on the error of denying the given thing altogether. In short, to categorically deny all things—designations and referents alike—is an extreme view which according to Asaṅga is much worse than the first defined above. He soon comments upon why this is so.

> Thus, if the aggregates of form exist, then the designation "person" is valid. But if they do not, the designation "person" is groundless. Attaching a verbal designation to the dharmas form, etc., and to the bare given thing of form, etc., is valid when they are existent *(sat)*. When they are not existent, the attaching of a verbal designation is groundless. And again, if there is no given thing present to be designated, then since there is no foundation, there is also no designation.
>
> Therefore, certain persons who have heard the abstruse sūtra passages associated with the Mahāyāna and associated with profound voidness, and that evince only an indirect meaning *(ābhiprāyikārtha)*, do not understand the meaning of the teaching as it really is *(yathābhūta)*. Those ones, imagining it superficially *(ayoniśa)*, thus have views posited merely by logic, without cogency, and speak as follows: "All this reality is just designation only. And whoever sees accordingly, that one sees rightly." According to those, the given thing itself, which is the foundation for designation, is lacking. But if this were so, no designations would occur at all! How should reality, then, come to be solely designation?

These two passages may be seen as constituting Asaṅga's definitive rebuttal to those who would misconstrue *śūnyatā* to be nothingness. Such a position is untenable for Asaṅga. Stated simply, "there is no this without that; that not being, this also is not." (It is precisely in the matter of the *relativity* of śūnyatā that Asaṅga and Nāgārjuna agree.)

Again, some persons who misunderstand the meaning of śūnyatā claim that nothing exists except names, i.e., "no things exist, only names." The major thrust of Asaṅga's arguments both here and in the exegesis has been to demonstrate the *mutual dependence* of names and things. Now, whatever is dependent does not partake of ultimate reality. Hence it is incorrect to assume that one dependent thing (i.e., designation) should exist in its own right.

But Asaṅga simultaneously argues another, more important, position here. Namely, he refutes the idea that one can completely deny the *vastu* (i.e., here the *paratantra* nature). Those who have "misunderstood" the true purport of the Mahāyāna teaching of śūnyatā suppose that it means the denial of all things, all vastus; but such ones misunderstand what part of the paratantra nature is to be denied and what part is not! Asaṅga's position is based upon the three svabhāvas. His exegesis (at 24b.8) states: "The meaning of all the provisional-meaning *sūtrāntas* is guided by the Three Natures. One should understand the meaning as the Tathāgata has stated it in innumerable ways in terms of the Three Natures, in its true significance; and as the bodhisattvas possessed of his Teaching have explained it in its true significance."

Accordingly, the undiscriminating, blanket denial of the *paratantra* nature prevents one from ever arriving at knowledge of ultimate reality (i.e., of the perfected, *pariniṣpanna* nature) since it leaves one stranded in nihilism. This second rebuttal, therefore, is aimed at those "insiders" (here, Nāgārjuna's followers) who misconstrue śūnyatā to mean the complete denial of the relative nature, as well as the imaginary nature. It also clearly voices Asaṅga's objection to the "two truths" theory, namely, that it is insufficient as a soteriological device *(upāya)*.

How can designations (imaginary nature) alone constitute ultimate reality *(pariniṣpanna)*? Designations arise when there are things present, and vice-versa. These are mutually dependent. When one recognizes this *mutual dependence*—which one does only when one accepts the existence in some way of *both* dependent components—one is getting close to the proper understanding of śūnyatā.

Moreover the passage from Asaṅga's exegesis just above points to a key feature of the Yogācārin approach to the issue of Buddhist hermeneutics. As mentioned previously, Mahāyāna Buddhism recognizes three phases of Buddhist philosophical development (the so-called "three turnings of the wheel of the Doctrine"), according to which the Yogācāra is judged the latest and, by implication, the most advanced. This strategem of the "three turnings" as a hermeneutical device is set forth in the *Saṃdhinirmocana sūtra,* a sūtra known to have been very highly regarded by Asaṅga. Now the chief problem of meaning and interpretation with regard to the Mahāyāna scriptures pertains to the Buddha's statements about emptiness *(śūnyatā)*. Asaṅga's exegesis here voices the hermeneutical judgement that all the sūtras—whether preached by the Buddha in a direct and explicit *(nītartha)* way or in a veiled and indirect *(neyārtha)* way—may be correctly understood only by employing the schema of the Yogācāra's "three nature" theory; and this particularly because the practitioner is thereby insulated against nihilism.

Accordingly, they deny both these two, reality as well as designation. One should understand that the denial of both reality and designation is the position of the chief nihilist *(pradhāna nāstika)*. Because his views are like this, the nihilist is not to be spoken with and not to be associated with by those intelligent ones *(vijña)* who live the pure life *(brahmacārin)*. Such a one, i.e., the nihilist, brings disaster even unto himself, and worldly ones who follow his view also fall into misfortune. In connection with this, the Lord has declared:

> Indeed, better it is for a being to have the view of a "person" than for one to have wrongly conceptualized voidness.

And why? Because men who have the view of a "person" are deluded only with respect to a single knowable, but they do not deny all knowables. And not for that reason alone would they be born among hell-beings.

Nor should another bring disaster to the seeker of Dharma, the seeker of liberation from suffering, nor deceive him. Rather, he should establish him in righteousness *(dharma)* and in Truth *(satya)*, and he should not be lax concerning the points of instruction. Because of the nihilist's wrongly conceptualized voidness, he is confused with respect to the knowable given thing of dharmas to the point of denying all knowables; and on that account one does get born among hell-beings. The nihilist would bring disaster to the righteous man, the seeker of liberation from suffering, and he would become lax

> concerning the points of instruction. Therefore, denying the given thing as it really is, he has strayed far from our Dharma-Vinaya.

The passages are for the most part self-explanatory. The extreme nihilist brings disaster to himself as well as others because, denying all things, he *destroys the moral precepts,* practices a totally hedonistic life-style conducive only to rebirths among hell-beings. Such behavior is completely the opposite of disciplined practice aimed at liberation. Hence, one treading the bodhisattva path should beware of such a one. Moreover, the passages indicate the great danger of misconstruing *śūnyatā* to mean nothingness. Though, according to Buddhist doctrine, having the view of a "person"—that is, assuming the independent existence of an individual "self"—is a mistaken view to be corrected, nevertheless, as the quotation makes clear, to have such a view is less dangerous than to have a mistaken notion about the true meaning of *śūnyatā.*

> Again, how is voidness wrongly conceptualized? There are some śramaṇas, as well as brāhmaṇas, who do not agree *(necchati)* concerning "owing to what there is a void"; nor do they agree concerning "that which is void." But such formulations as these are evidence of what is said to be "voidness wrongly conceptualized." And why? Voidness is logical when one thing is void of another because of that [other's] absence and because of the presence of the void thing itself. But how and for what reason would the void come to be from universal ab-

sence [*sarva-abhāvāt,* i.e., from complete nonexistence]? Hence, the conception of voidness these describe is not valid. And therefore, in this manner voidness is wrongly conceptualized.

Though brief, the above passage is quite important, since in it Asaṅga refutes the position of those who claim to propound the doctrine of śūnyatā but who, according to Asaṅga's system, have not well considered the cogency of their argument. The Sanskrit of the passage is very terse. It reads (beginning at "There are some"):

yaḥ kaścic chramaṇo vā brāhmaṇo vā
tac ca necchati yena śūnyaṃ.
tad api necchati yat śūnyaṃ.
iyaṃ evaṃ-rūpā durgṛhīta śūnyatety
ucyate, tat kasya hetoḥ.
yena hi śūnyaṃ. tad a-sad-bhāvāt.
yac ca śūnyaṃ. tad sad-bhāvāc
chūnyatā yujyeta.

The crux of the passage turns on the two phrases *yena śūnyaṃ* and *yat śūnyaṃ.* Literally, those ones do not agree concerning "owing to what *(yena)* there is a void"; nor do they agree concerning "that which is *(yat)* void." The passage is aimed at further explicating the absurdity of the extreme nihilist's position—for such a one claims to understand voidness but at the same time holds to the nonexistence of "absolutely everything." Asaṅga asserts here that any claim to universal denial *(sarva-abhāvāt)* precludes the possibility of voidness.

This is a key example for illustrating the "flavor" of the Yogācāra position and of the three natures theory. For

Asaṅga, the term "voidness" is only applicable in a context in which there is an existent thing to which it applies. The void thing *(vastu)* must be present in some way in order for the assertion that it is void (of something) to be valid. If no such thing is present, then the designation "voidness" is groundless. But the nihilists wish to say that absolutely everything is nonexistent and nonpresent. So saying, according to Asaṅga, they deny voidness as well.

Moreover, the argument as put forth by Asaṅga is aimed specifically at refuting those who would deny the *paratantra* nature. Asaṅga says to such a one: You deny the self-existent entity. In this, we agree with you. You also deny the non-self-existent entity (i.e., the *paratantra),* but in this denial we can not agree with you—for if you say that all self-existence is nonexistent, then certainly your claim *proves* that non-self-existence exists! And this is Asaṅga's main point, namely, *voidness does exist.*

An example may be helpful in illustrating the passage's meaning. Take a book. Now, a self-existent book is not present, i.e., does not exist. Why? Because it is *dependent* (on a number of various causes and conditions, viz., its author, the press that printed it, the paper, thread, and ink that went into producing it, etc.). Consequently, it is not self-existent, not having caused its own production. But being not self-existent, it is dependent, i.e., not existing in its own right. Now, owing to what is the book void (of self-existence)? Owing to the very fact of its dependence. But were someone to claim that both self-existence and non-self-existence were nonexistent, how should that one ever presume to discuss the book, let alone its voidness, at all? The book, it should be clear, is in Asaṅga's system the non-*self*-existent but dependently existent entity, i.e., the paratantra nature.

Now, how is voidness rightly conceptualized? Wherever and in whatever place something is not, one rightly observes that [place] to be void of that [thing]. Moreover, whatever remains in that place one knows *(prajanati)* as it really is, that "here there is an existent." This is said to be engagement with voidness as it really is and without waywardness. For example, when a given thing, as indicated, is termed "form," etc., there is no dharma identical to the verbal designation "form" and so on. Hence, whenever a dharma is termed "form" etc., that given thing is void of identity with the verbal designation "form," etc. Then what remains in that place when a given thing is termed "form," etc.? As follows: just the basis *(āśraya)* of the verbal designation "form," etc. When one knows both those as they really are—namely, that there is just a given thing and there is just a designation for just a given thing—then he neither affirms the existence of what is nonexistent nor denies what is existent. He neither makes it in excess nor makes it in deficiency. He neither minimizes nor adds.

And when he knows Suchness, as it really is, with its inexpressible essential nature, as it really is, this is called "voidness rightly conceptualized," and called "well-discerned right insight." By this means and others consistent with demonstration-and-proof reasoning, he will come to judge that the essential nature of all dharmas is inexpressible.

The above passages state Asaṅga's position quite clearly. For him, voidness is grasped "rightly" by that one who sees with the Middle Path mode of viewing, i.e., who neither exaggerates nor minimizes reality as it really is. He neither denies nor affirms *in toto.* Rather, he sees what he sees as "just that" and he knows that it is possible for a thing to exist in such a way that it is neither totally existent nor totally nonexistent. He views all things as being neither of these two extremes. Consequently, he comes to judge the essential nature of all things as being, in fact, inexpressible.

In the next passages Asaṅga cites scriptural authority for the above philosophical discussion, and for the position taken here.

[III]

> Moreover, one should understand that all dharmas have an inexpressible essential nature from the scriptures *(āgama)* of a trustworthy person *(āpta).* This very meaning was expressed by the Lord through an elucidating verse *(gāthābhigīta)* in the "Discourse on Transference in Phenomenal Life" *(Bhavasaṃkrāntisūtra):*
>
> Indeed by whatsoever name whatsoever dharma is mentioned, that dharma is not found therein. For that is the true nature *(dharmatā)* of all dharmas.

With this passage Asaṅga begins a section that offers scriptural authority for the proper understanding of "voidness" as outlined above. The first sūtra cited, the *Bhavasaṃkrānti-sūtra* (Tib. *srid pa 'pho ba'i mdo*), is mentioned in the *Mahāvyutpatti* (see item 1379), where it is said to be one of the earliest Mahāyāna scriptures. In addition to being cited here by Asaṅga, the *Bhavasaṃkrānti* is alluded to by Candrakīrti in his *Madhyamakāvatara.* Its importance is further verified by the fact that there exist whole commentaries on the sūtra which are attributed to Asaṅga and Nāgārjuna (i.e., the *Bhavasaṃkrānti-ṭīkā* and the *Bhavasaṃkrāntiśāstra,* respectively).

A rather short sūtra in length, the *Bhavasaṃkrānti-sūtra* takes the form of a dialogue between the Buddha and Bimbisāra, King of Magadha. Its main subject matter revolves around the explanation of how there can be rebirth, or more accurately in the context of the sūtra, transmigration *(saṃkrānti),* in light of the doctrine of *anātman,* nonself.

The format of the sūtra is as follows: During the first, prose section, the Buddha explains to Bimbisāra how rebirth takes place by virtue of actions which are only momentary. To accomplish this, he gives a detailed explanation based on the example of a dream. Then, at the end of this prose section, there are enumerated seven verses—the one quoted here by Asaṅga being the second such verse.

The verses of this sūtra are additionally notable since they propound one of the earliest Mahāyāna statements of the Two Truths (i.e., *saṃvṛtisatya* and *pāramārthasatya*). For fuller details and translation of the sūtra together with the two commentaries, see N. A. Sastri's translation of the *Bhavasaṃkrāntisūtra.*

Asaṅga's own explanation of the verse, immediately following, eloquently interprets it.

How does this verse elucidate our very meaning? When a dharma has the name "form" and so on, whatever the name be, i.e., "form," etc., by means of that name the dharmas are referred to with the names "form," etc., whether form or feeling and so on, up to Nirvāṇa. But the dharmas having those names "form," etc., are themselves not identical with the designations "form," etc. Nor is there any dharma found outside of those that is identical to "form," etc. Again, for those dharmas having the names "form," etc., one should understand that what does exist there in the ultimate sense, with an inexpressible meaning, is the true mode *(dharmatā)* of essential nature. And it was spoken by the Lord in the discourse treating the categories of dharmas [the *Arthavargīya*]:

> Whatever conventions there be among the worldly, all those the Muni does not take up. And verily not participating, how could he indulge, since he takes no pleasure in what is seen or heard?

The *Arthavargīya-sūtra* (Tib. *don gyi sde tshan dag mdo)* exists in the Pāli Canon under the title *Aṭṭhakavagga.* There it is found as the thirteenth *sutta* of a larger collection entitled the *Mahāviyuhasutta* in the fourth section of the famed *Sutta Nipāta.* The verse cited here is the third of thirteen verses comprising the *Aṭṭhakavagga.* In the Pāli version it runs as follows:

> *Yā kāc' imā sammutiyo puthujjā; sabbā va etā na upeti vidvā; anūpayo so upayaṃ kim eyya diṭṭhe sute khantim akubbamāno.*

Though the Sanskrit version of this sūtra is no longer extant, we know that it did exist not only because Asaṅga's quotation is in Sanskrit, but also because a Chinese translation (by a translator Tche-K'ien, done between the years 223 and 253 A.D.) was made from an original Sanskrit version, according to Lamotte *(Histoire du Bouddhisme Indien,* p. 173).

The *Sutta Nipāta* is itself revered as representing one of the oldest strata of Buddhist literature. That Asaṅga quotes from this particular sūtra testifies to both his reverence for and his knowledge of the ancient literature, as well as to his belief that such ideas as he is here expounding are found, in fact, in that literature.

How does this verse elucidate our very meaning? Whatever be the designations, such as "form," etc., applied to a dharma of form, etc., those are said to be "conventions." He does not accept that dharmas are identical with those designations. In this respect, he does not accept those conventions. And why? Because his view is neither that of exaggeration *(samāropa)* nor of underestimation *(apavada)*. Now because he does not have a wayward *(viparyāsa)* view, he is said to not participate. Thus not participating, how is he to indulge? Without that wayward view, he neither affirms nor denies that given thing; and not indulging, he rightly sees in the knowable what is to be seen of it. And what he hears spoken of the knowable was indeed heard of it. In regard to what is seen and heard, he neither originates nor increases craving. Not otherwise would he rid himself of the object of consciousness *(ālambana)* and dwell with equanimity; and having equanimity, he does not create desire *(kāntim)*.

The Muni (referring here both to a sage of the silent meditative path and to the Buddha himself) does not take up worldly conventions. Hence, unlike ordinary beings, he neither exaggerates *(samāropa)* nor underestimates *(apavada)* reality.

The term *viparyāsa,* rendered here as "wayward view," is traditionally in Buddhism applied to four general misconceptions of ordinary beings, namely: (1) taking as permanent what is really impermanent; (2) taking as self-possessing what is without self; (3) taking as pure what is impure; and (4) taking as pleasant what is really painful. Asaṅga's exegesis (at 22b.3) adds a fifth "wayward view" which he defines as "taking the imaginary or imputed nature as the object *(nimitta = vastu)* itself."

Not having these wayward views, the Muni "neither affirms nor denies that given thing." Hence, experiencing the inexpressible essential nature of the given thing, "he rightly sees in it what is to be seen of it." This passage also makes clear that it is only by "not participating" through attachment, longing, or expectation, that one *ceases to cling* to an object and/or to its designation, thereby attaining equanimity.

> And again, such was declared by the Lord in the discourse beginning with the story of the "Saṃtha Kātyāyana." In this account, the monk having the title "Saṃtha" meditates neither upon the base *(āyatana)* earth, water, fire, nor wind; neither upon the bases space, perception, or nothing-at-all, nor ideation nor nonideation; neither upon this world nor the other; neither upon the sun nor the moon; nor upon what is seen, heard, thought, perceived,

obtained, striven for, inquired about, or concluded about by the mind. None of these does he employ as a meditative base. Now since he does not meditate upon the base earth, etc., nor all the rest, upon what does he meditate? Here, for the saṃtha monk, whatever the idea *(saṃjñā)* of "earth" regarding earth, that idea is lost *(vibhūta)*. Whatever the idea of "water" with regard to water, and with regard to all the rest, that idea is lost. Thus this monk meditates, not using earth as a meditative base nor any of the others. Using none of them at all as a meditative base, he meditates. Therefore do all the gods along with Indra, along with the Īśānas, and along with Prajāpati, bow down near the monk thus meditating, saying,

> Salutations to this noble man. Salutations to the best of men. To you for whom there is nothing further to know, resorting to what will you meditate?

Again, how does this sūtra verse elucidate our very intent? For given things named "earth," etc., "earth" and so on are only nominal designations. For those given things named "earth," etc., the idea of them arises with exaggeration, or the idea of them arises with underestimation. The idea with "exaggeration" posits the essential nature of the given thing as consisting of that name; and the idea with "underestimation" posits the destruction of the ultimate basis of the given thing itself. When these two erroneous views are abandoned and eliminated, the idea of any meditative base is said to be "lost."

Dutt's Sanskrit edition of the *Bodhisattvabhūmi,* p. 49, places the *Saṃtha Kātyāyana-sūtra* in the *Aṅguttara-Nikāya,* V, 224.28–329.19. A *saṃtha* is a meditator noted for his steadfast concentration.

The *āyatanas* (Tib. *skye mched)* or "bases" are traditionally enumerated as twelve and may be called factors of consciousness. Comprised of the six sense objects and the six sense organs, they are fundamental elements of Buddhist epistemology. Here the term is also made synonymous with the various *kasinas,* or the so-called ten meditative "devices," and meditative objects of all kinds from gross to extremely subtle "mental supports" (i.e., *ālambanas).*

Because he does not cling to any object nor to its designation, it is said that the idea of such things is "lost" to him. Thus he meditates using no meditative object, i.e., not one that can be determined through speech. Being inexpressible, it is said to be "lost."

The term *vibhūta* is interesting here because of the unusual usage on the part of Asaṅga, where *vi-* is here made to function as a privative in conjunction with the root *bhū.* Professor Wayman noticed this in Asaṅga's *Śrāvakabhūmi* context. (See Wayman's *Analysis,* p. 57, where he defines *vibhāvanā* as "leaving off the intense contemplation" [*bhāvanā*].) Monier-Williams was apparently unaware of this usage. See his entry for *vibhūta* in his *Sanskrit-English Dictionary,* p. 978. Apparently, there is a tradition among Yogācārins for using conjunctions of "*vi*" and "*bhū*" in this way, for the same can be observed in the *Mahāyānasūtrālaṅkāra.*

Names, we are told, generate ideas of the things named which are either exaggerations or underestimations of those things. The meditator who recognizes this distorting character of names, abandons them (becoming, if you will, a "silent one," a muni) and their concomitant distorting ideas. Hence he meditates upon "nothing at all."

The final portion of the above passage gives perhaps the clearest formulation of Asaṅga's view of the Middle Path. That is, it is the Path which avoids (1) positing that the essential nature of the given thing consists of its name; and (2) positing the destruction of the ultimate basis of the given thing.

> Therefore from the Scriptures and also from the Tathāgata's supreme lineage of trustworthy successors, one should understand that all dharmas have an inexpressible essential nature. Now, since all dharmas have thus inexpressible essential nature, why is expression applicable at all? Verily, because without expression, the inexpressible true nature could not be told to others, nor heard by others. And if it were neither spoken nor heard, then the inexpressible essential nature could not become known. Therefore, expression is applicable for producing knowledge through hearing.

[IV]

Precisely because that Suchness is not thoroughly known *(aparijñātatva)*, the eight kinds of discursive thought *(vikalpa)* arise for immature beings *(bāla)* and operate so as to create the three bases *(trivastu)*, which further produce the receptacle worlds *(bhājanaloka)* of all sentient beings. The eight are as follows: (1) discursive thought concerning essential nature; (2) discursive thought concerning particularity; (3) discursive thought concerning grasping whole shapes; (4) discursive thought concerning "I"; (5) discursive thought concerning "mine"; (6) discursive thought concerning the agreeable; (7) discursive thought concerning the disagreeable; and (8) discursive thought contrary to both these.

Here begins the last major section of the chapter. With the above passage Asaṅga begins his thorough analysis of discursive thought. He tells us that there are eight distinct kinds of such thought and that these eight produce three things (here "bases") that further engender all the realms of *saṃsāra.* Here "receptacle worlds," *bhājanaloka* (Tib. *snod kyi 'jig rten),* refers to the five (in the Hīnayāna) and six (in the Mahāyāna) *gatis,* or destinies which comprise *saṃsāra,* i.e., (1) the *naraka,* or hell (beings), (2) *pretas* (hungry ghosts), (3) animals, (4) humans, (5) *devas,* or gods, and (6) *asuras,* demigods.

The *vastu* of *trivastu* (Tib. *gźi gsum)* has a broader connotation in these passages than before. Hence, it is rendered by "base." While in fact the *first* of these "three bases" is identical with the *vastu* rendered throughout as "given thing," the perceived object (its *paratantra* nature), with regard to the other two cases its meaning is more akin to "base" or "basis" in the sense of what underlies, supports, or produces phenomena as they are perceived. This broader connotation should be kept in mind while reading this section.

There follows a description of how the eight *vikalpas* produce the three bases, or more precisely, which *vikalpas* generate which base. We learn that discursive thought about essential nature, particularity, and "whole shapes" *(piṇḍagrāha-vikalpa)* is responsible for producing the base (here, *vastu* = "given thing," referent) which is then named and becomes the foundation for further discursive proliferation.

The discursive thoughts about "I" and "mine" produce the base which is the view of "self" and of "what belongs to self." Lastly, discursive thought about what is agreeable, what is disagreeable, or what, being neither, is neutral, produces variously the three primary *kleśas,* desire, hatred, and delusion. That is, it seems discursive thought about the agreeable is responsible for engendering desire; about the disagreeable, hatred; and about neither, delusion. These three kleśas, it should be remembered, are the very hub of the "wheel of saṃsāra." Further, Asaṅga tells us, the three bases are intimately connected, such that the view of "self" has a support only when there is the view of an object (i.e., of "a base which is named") in contradistinction to which it is defined—a self-other, subject-object dualism. And the three kleśas of desire, hatred, and delusion are possible only when there are the ideas of "self" and of "what belongs to self." Hence, since discursive thought and its proliferation—which produce objects, ideas of "I" and "mine," desire and hatred, etc.—are responsible for the evolution of all the realms of suffering, it is the bodhisattva's obligation to well understand the nature and workings of discursive thought.

Further, these eight kinds of discursive thought create what three bases? The discursive thought concerning essential nature, the discursive thought concerning particularity, and the discursive thought concerning grasping whole shapes, these three engender the [perceivable] base which is named "form," etc., i.e., the base which serves as the foundation of discursive proliferation and as its mental support *(ālambana)*. With that [perceivable] base as its foundation, discursive thought—saturated with words, ideas, and names and enveloped in words, ideas, and names—proliferates and ranges on that base in many ways.

Of these eight, the discursive thought concerning "I" and the discursive thought concerning "mine" engender the reifying view *(satkāyadṛṣṭi)*, and the root of all other views, namely: the root of pride *(māna)*, the root of egoism *(asmi-māna)*, and the root of all other self-centered views.

Among those eight, discursive thought concerning the agreeable and the disagreeable, as well as discursive thought which is contrary to both these, engender, according to the circumstances, desire, hatred, or delusion *(rāgadveṣamoha)*.

Thus do these eight kinds of discursive thought serve to manifest the three kinds of bases, namely: (1) the [perceivable] base which serves as the foundation of discursive thought and its proliferation; (2) the base of the reifying view, egoism, and pride; and (3) the base of lust, hatred, and delusion. With regard to those, when the [perceivable] base of discursive thought together with proliferation exist, then the reifying view and the "I am" pride have a support; and when the reifying view and the "I am" pride exist, then lust, hatred, and delusion have a

> support. Further, these three bases explain completely the manifold evolution of all the worlds [of saṃsāra].

There follows now a detailed definition of each of the eight types of *vikalpa*. Discursive thought concerning essential nature posits the assumed nature or essence of its object. Discursive thought concerning particularity delineates specifics and posits distinctions. Discursive thought concerning grasping whole shapes posits the lumping or grouping together of individual dharmas into wholes, the compounding of separate characteristics into a single unit. This is exactly the process of reification in which separate, individual dharmas are viewed as lumped together and are then named. Such thought formulates universals. When we do this with the "aggregates," we, mistakenly, reify a "self," an "I," where in truth there is none. That discursive thought concerning "I" and "mine" generates the ideas of "self" and of "what belongs to self"—these latter being responsible for the mistaken notion that objects are truly existent as perceived by the "self"; and, as mentioned before, discursive thought about what is agreeable, disagreeable, or neutral causes, according to the circumstances, the three kleśas.

> 1. Among those eight, what is discursive thought concerning essential nature? It is that discursive thought which designates "form," etc., when there is a given thing of form, etc. This is said to be discursive thought concerning essential nature.
>
> 2. What is discursive thought concerning particularity? It is that discursive thought which, when

there is a given thing named "form," etc., thinks, "This has form," "This is formless," "This is shown," "This is not shown," "This has hindrance," "This is unhindered," "This is outflow," "This is not outflow," "This is compounded," "This is uncompounded," "virtuous," "unvirtuous," "indeterminate," "past," "future," "present"; and by way of immeasurable distinctions of the same category, whatever discursive thought is founded upon the discursive thought concerning essential nature, with the object of particularizing it, this is said to be discursive thought concerning particularity.

3. What is discursive thought concerning grasping whole shapes? When there is a given thing named "form," etc., whatever operates to grasp whole shapes with respect to the multiple dharmas taken together, adding to given things nominal designations like "self," "life," and "sentient being"; and adding nominal designations like "house," "army," and "forest," "food," "drink," "conveyance," and "clothes," etc., this is said to be discursive thought concerning grasping whole shapes.

4.5. What is discursive thought concerning "I" and "mine"? When a given thing has outflow, is graspable, and for a long time has been familiar, clung to *(abhiniviṣṭa),* and thought of as "self" *(ātmata),* or as "what belongs to self" *(ātmīyata),* so by intimacy with that errant way of conceptualizing, discursive thought wrongly takes the given thing, which has arisen dependently, as having been placed there by one's own view. This is said to be discursive thought concerning "I" and "mine."

6. What is discursive thought concerning the agreeable? It is that discursive thought which has as its mental support a given thing which is pleasant and captivating to the mind.

7. What is discursive thought concerning the disagreeable? It is that discursive thought which has as its mental support a given thing which is unpleasant and revolting to the mind.

8. What is discursive thought which is contrary to both the agreeable and disagreeable? It is that discursive thought which has as its mental support a given thing which is neither pleasant nor unpleasant, neither captivating nor revolting to the mind.

And this whole process is composed of two elements only: discursive thought, and the given thing, which then becomes the mental support of discursive thought and the foundation of discursive thought. It should be understood that these two are mutually caused *(anyonya hetuka)* and without beginning in time. A previous discursive thought is the cause which generates a present given thing which, in turn, becomes the mental support of discursive thought. And again, the generated given thing which is the present mental support for discursive thought is the cause which generates the future discursive thought having that as its mental support.

Now, with respect to this, it is precisely from lack of understanding that the discursive thought of the present is the cause which generates the given thing in the future—and that this given thing in turn becomes the mental support of discursive thought in

> the future—that there is the inevitable *(niyata)* generation of discursive thought in the future, having that thing as its foundation and as its basis.

The above passages assert the mutual dependence of the discursive thought and the given thing. One might substitute "name" or "designation" for "discursive thought" here, as the idea is to point out that the one—be it name, designation, idea, thought, or what have you—is dependent upon the other. Asaṅga's exegesis devotes a good deal of space to providing interesting examples which show that this is so.

From such passages it can also be deduced that Asaṅga is no idealist, at least as this is understood in the tradition of Western philosophy, for clearly given things, or objects, exist as much as do names—in fact, according to the theory of the three natures, even more so. For Asaṅga, "idealism" would be associated with discursive thought, *vikalpa,* and hence with the distorting nature of conceptualization. As such it would be denounced rather than exalted by the Yogācāra school.

As we will be advised later, for the bodhisattva who thoroughly comprehends the nature and functioning of discursive thought, both the discursive thought and its base, the "given thing," simultaneously dissolve. Hence, far from advocating the superiority of thought over objects, Asaṅga's explication of śūnyatā and the Middle Path involves the cessation of both subject and object, both apprehender and thing apprehended. Only knowledge freed completely of discursive thought knows an object as it really is. This state of knowing, however, must be described as inexpressible, since when the object is seen as it really is, it is not seen *as* an object, i.e., as separate or apart from the seer. But the seer too dissolves into the seen—because the object is seen as it really is. Hence, not idealism, but a state of intimate, inexpressible knowledge of reality is aimed at.

But now how does thorough knowledge *(parijñāna)* of discursive thought arise? It arises by means of the four thorough investigations *(paryeṣaṇās)* and by means of the four kinds of knowing precisely and in detail *(yathābhūtaparijñānas)*. What are the four thorough investigations? They are the investigation of the name, the investigation of the given thing, the investigation of the designations for essential nature, and the investigation of the designations for particularity.

The four *paryeṣaṇas* (Tib. *yoṅs su tshol ba)* and the four *yathābhūtaparijñānas* (Tib. *yaṅ dag pa ji lta ba bźin du yoṅs su śes pa)* are technical investigations falling within the realm of insight-meditations (i.e., *vipaśyana)* and conducted by Buddhist practitioners. Asaṅga begins by discussing the four *paryeṣaṇas,* or "thorough investigations." This same fourfold grouping is enumerated with explanations in Asaṅga's *Mahāyānasaṃgraha,* chapter 3, section 7. (See Lamotte's translation, vol. II, p. 161.)

Likewise, the four are treated in chapter 19, verse 47 of the *Mahāyānasūtrālaṅkāra* (the chapter there treats of the bodhisattva's qualities and is entitled the *Guṇādhikāra).* Sthiramati's commentary on this chapter, and this verse in particular, is interesting. His commentary (found in *PTT,* vol. 109, p. 98, folio 1) says:

"[This kind of] search is done at the time of the *ādhimuk-*

ticāryabhūmi" [i.e., that stage just before entering into the first bodhisattva stage]. Hence, these four searches can be done by the śrāvakas and pratyekabuddhas. It may be that the four, at least according to Sthiramati, are equivalent to the four *nirvedha-bhagīyas,* or "analytic penetrations."

Sthiramati's statements suggest a clear distinction between these four *paryeṣaṇas* and the four *yathābhūtaparijñānas* by suggesting that the former may be practiced by those of the two lesser vehicles but that the latter are the province solely of the bodhisattvas.

There follow the characterizations of these "thorough investigations." In each case the entity being investigated is to be recognized as "just that," with neither exaggeration or minimization. The investigator recognizes that even though names are "just names" and things are "just things," designations for essential nature and for particularity arise when the two, i.e., names and things, are conjoined.

> With respect to these, investigation of the name means that the bodhisattva sees with regard to a name that it is just a name. Likewise, with regard to a given thing, seeing that it is just a given thing is the investigation of the given thing. With respect to designations for essential nature, clearly seeing those as just designations for essential nature is the investigation of designations for essential nature; and with regard to designations for particularity, seeing those as just designations for particularity is the investigation of designations for particularity. He sees names and given things as having distinct characteristics *(bhinna lakṣaṇa)* and as having connected characteristics *(anuśliṣṭa lakṣaṇa);* and

he realizes *(prativídhyati)* that designations for essential nature and designations for particularity are based upon the connected characteristics of the name and the given thing.

What are the four kinds of knowing precisely, in detail? They are knowing in detail the investigated name, the investigated given thing, the designations for essential nature, and the designations for particularity—knowing all these precisely, in detail.

Having viewed the four entities in a general way and having concluded that each is "just that," Asaṅga now describes the advanced practice for a bodhisattva of coming to penetrate each of these "precisely, in detail."

According, again, to Sthiramati's commentary, these four occur in the first bodhisattva stage. Sthiramati writes: "The bodhisattva now searches the character of voidness" (i.e., *stoṅ pa ñid mtshan ñid)*. In folio 5, he describes the four as follows: "(1) knowing . . . that all names are *avastuka* [i.e., groundless and without actual referents] and void; (2) knowing . . . all *vastus* are without essential nature and void; (3) knowing . . . all *svalakṣaṇas* [i.e., individual characteristics] are without essential nature and void; and (4) knowing . . . all dharmas arising and ceasing [*sāmānya-lakṣaṇas,* or dharmas with "connected characteristics"] are without essential nature and void."

Therefore, the bodhisattva on the first stage comes to "know precisely, in detail" the non-self of the dharmas *(dharmanairātmya)*. The four *yathābhūtaparijñānas* are given an explication quite similar to that of our chapter in the *Mahāyānasaṃgraha,* 3.8.

What is knowing precisely, in detail, the investigated name? You should know that the bodhisattva, having investigated name as name only, knows that name precisely; to wit, he determines that "This name is the linguistic unit *(artha)* for a given thing"; likewise "the linguistic unit for conceptualizing, the linguistic unit for viewing, and the linguistic unit for attributing *(upacāra)*." If, for a given thing ordinarily conceived of as form, etc., a name "form" is not decided upon, no one would thus conceive of that given thing as form; and not conceiving it, he would not exaggerate or cling to it. And not clinging to it, he could not express it. Thus he knows it precisely, in detail. This is said to be knowing the investigated name precisely, in detail.

What is knowing precisely, in detail, the investigated given thing? For any given thing, the bodhisattva, having investigated it as given thing only, sees that that given thing, while conceived of as "form," etc., and while associated with all the expressions [for it], is in itself inexpressible. This is the second knowing in detail, namely, knowing precisely, in detail, the investigated given thing.

Coming to know the nature of the name as it really is, i.e., that it is a linguistic unit which facilitates discursive thought and upon which discursive thought operates and proliferates, the bodhisattva recognizes that it is on account of name that conceptualizing is possible, that opinions, attributions, and embellishments arise. Likewise, the bodhisattva recognizes that were it not for names, exaggeration and underestimation could not operate and hence clinging would be forced to cease. Recognizing this as the true nature of name, he is said to know it precisely, in detail.

What is knowing the given thing precisely? That is knowing that in itself, i.e., in its ultimate *(paramārthika)* sense, the given thing is inexpressible, and completely disassociated from discursive thought. It is the "nondiscursive" knowable.

> What is knowing precisely, in detail, the investigated designations for essential nature? It is that knowing whereby the bodhisattva, with regard to a given thing conceived of as "form," etc., after having investigated its designations for essential nature as designations only, knows and well knows in detail that in designations relating to that given thing there is only the mere semblance of essential nature, and that in truth essential nature is lacking there. For him, seeing that "essential nature" as but a magical creation, a reflected image, an echo, a hallucination, the moon's reflection in the waters, a dream and an illusion, he knows that this semblance is not made up of that essential nature. This is the third knowing precisely, in detail, which is the sphere of most profound knowledge *(sugambhīrārtha gocara)*.
>
> What is the knowing precisely, in detail, the investigated designations for particularity? It is that knowing whereby the bodhisattva, after having investigated the designations for particularity as designations only attached to the given things called "form," etc., sees designations for particularity as having a not-two meaning. The given thing is neither completely present nor completely absent

> [neither existent nor nonexistent]. It is not present, since it is not "perfected" *(pariniṣpannatva),* owing to its having an expressible "self." And it is not altogether absent, since in fact it is determined to have an inexpressible essence. Thus from the stance of absolute truth *(paramārthasatya),* it is not formed *(rūpī),* yet from the stance of relative truth *(saṃvṛtisatya)* it is not formless, since form is attributed to it. As with presence and absence, or formed and formless, just so is whatever is shown or not shown, and so forth. All the enumerations of designations for particularity should be understood in just this same manner. He [the bodhisattva] knows in detail, as having a not-two meaning, whatever be the designations for particularity. This is knowing precisely, in detail, the investigated designations for particularity.

The bodhisattva comes to realize that—from the relative point of view—only the semblance of essential nature is indicated by designations for essential nature, and that from the absolute point of view, no essential nature whatsoever is to be found in them. This knowledge is characterized as being "most profound."

Here Asaṅga lists only a few similes instructive for the bodhisattva viewing the relative nature (i.e., the *paratantra* aspect) of designations for essential nature and their respective given things. His exegesis provides a much longer list. The passage here is interesting because it makes clear that similes are only applicable to the *relative* aspect of things or relationships. They are not applicable to ultimate nature.

With regard to designations for particularity, the bodhisattva knows these "precisely, in detail," when he/she recognizes that such designations serve only to posit extreme characterizations. Since they serve to distinguish distinct attributes, claiming that a given thing is wholly either this or that, such designations always distort reality. The bodhisattva thus correctly knows these as they really are when, seeing their nature, he/she views them as having a "not-two" meaning, and as referring to a reality which, in truth, cannot be expressed in a cut-and-dried fashion.

Asaṅga ends this section by urging on the bodhisattva. He assures him/her that the evolution of saṃsāra and its consequent sufferings will cease together with the discursive thought that engendered it for one who has mastered these four kinds of "knowing precisely, in detail."

> Now it should be understood that those eight kinds of errant *(mithyā)* discursive thought which belong to immature beings and which engender the three bases and cause the continual return to the world, operate through weakness of, and non-engagement with, these four kinds of knowing precisely, in detail. Moreover, from errant discursive thought defilement arises; from defilement, circling in saṃsāra; from circling in saṃsāra, the consequences of saṃsāra, i.e., the sufferings of birth, old age, disease, and death.
>
> But whenever the bodhisattva resorts to the four kinds of knowing precisely, in detail, he knows the eight kinds of discursive thought. And because of his right knowledge, in this lifetime *(dṛṣṭe dharme)* there is no generation, now or in the future, of a given thing associated with proliferation which

> could serve as a mental support and as a foundation for discursive thought. And because discursive thought does not arise, there is no generation in the future of a given thing having that as its support. Thus for him that discursive thought, along with the given thing, ceases *(nirodha)*. This should be understood as the cessation of all proliferation.

Above Asaṅga gives the final characterization of the goal sought by the bodhisattva, namely, the complete cessation of discursive thought along with the accompanying given thing. It is the state of supreme knowledge of reality, i.e., knowledge completely freed of discursive thought *(nirvikalpa jñāna)*.

> Therefore, one should understand the complete cessation of proliferation as the bodhisattva's "Parinirvāṇa of the Great Vehicle." Because of the complete purity of his knowledge, now the sphere of the most splendid knowledge of reality, in this lifetime that bodhisattva attains the mastery of power everywhere *(sarvatra vaśitāprāpti)*; for example, he attains the mastery of multiform magical creation *(nirmāṇa)* owing to the magical power *(ṛddhi)* of creating; of multiform transformation *(pariṇāma)* owing to the magical power of transformation; of knowledge of all knowables; of remaining in the world as long as he wishes, and of departing from the world at his pleasure, without hindrance.

The bodhisattva who has attained to *nirvikalpa jñāna* comes to possess also what is termed the "mastery of power everywhere" *(sarvatra vaśitāprāpti;* Tib. *thams cad la dbaṅ thob pa rñed pa)*. According to the *Daśabhūmika* and other Mahāyāna treatises, the bodhisattva of the eighth stage acquires ten *vaśitas,* or powers, though Asaṅga here gives only an abbreviated list. Dayal's *Bodhisattva Doctrine,* pp. 140–41, describes the ten as follows:

1) *Āyur-vaśitā* (power of longevity). A bodhisattva has sovereignty over the length of life. He can prolong it to an immeasurable number of *kalpas* (aeons).

2) *Ceto-(Citta)-vaśitā.* He has sovereignty over the mind, as he has acquired the knowledge of an infinite number of *samādhis* (modes of Concentration).

3) *Pariṣkāra-vaśitā.* He has the mastery of Equipment, and he knows all the arrangements and adornments of all the worlds and universes.

4) *Karma-vaśitā.* He has sovereignty over Action, as he comprehends the consequences of deeds at the proper time.

5) *Upapatti-vaśitā.* He has mastery over Birth, as he understands the origin of all the worlds and universes.

6) *Adhimukti-vaśitā.* He has sovereignty over Faith (or Aspiration), as he sees well all the Buddhas of all the worlds and universes.

7) *Praṇidhāna-vaśitā.* He has mastery over all the Vows, as he sees well the time for Enlightenment in any buddha-field according to his desire.

8) *Ṛddhi-vaśitā.* He is lord of the wonder-working Power, as he sees well the marvels of all the buddha-fields.

9) *Dharma-vaśitā.* He has mastery over the Doctrine, as he beholds the light of the source of the Doctrine in the beginning, the middle and the end.

10) *Jñāna-vaśitā.* He comprehends thoroughly the attributes of a Buddha, viz., his Powers, his Grounds of Self-confidence, his special exclusive attributes, and the principal marks and the minor signs on his body. Therefore he is the Lord of Knowledge.

Thus that one, with that mastery of power, is best of and incomparable among all beings. And you should understand that the bodhisattva has five superior benefits *(anuśaṃsā)* which control in all circumstances, namely: (1) he attains supreme peace of mind, because he attains the tranquil stations *(vihārapraśāntatayā)* and not by reason of pacifying defilement; (2) his knowledge and vision with respect to all the sciences are unimpeded, extremely pure, and perfectly clear; (3) he is unwearied by his circling in saṃsāra for the sake of beings; (4) he understands all the speech with "veiled intention" *(saṃdhāya vacanāni)* of the Tathāgatas; and (5) because he is self-reliant, not depending on others, he is not led away from his zealous devotion *(adhimukti)* to the Great Vehicle.

In addition to the various magical powers *(ṛddhi)* attained by the bodhisattva who has comprehended the true nature of reality as it really is, there are five benefits *(anuśaṃsā)* that also are gained. Asaṅga enumerates these above.

In describing the first benefit the Sanskrit passage reads: *paramāṃ cittaśāṃtimanuprāpto bhavati vihārapraśaṃtatayā na kleśapraśāntatayā.* Professor Wayman has pointed out that *vihāra* here is equivalent to *bhūmi.* Hence, the "tranquil stations" mentioned here are equivalent to the bodhisattva stages. The peace and tranquillity resulting from pacifying the defilements (i.e. *kleśapraśāntataya)* would have been accomplished at an earlier stage in the bodhisattva's career. Hence the supremacy of the tranquillity experienced in the bhūmis is clearly implied.

The term *saṃdhāya vacanāni* (Tib. *ldem po'i ṅag)* has been rendered here as "speech with veiled intention" following the language of the *Saṃdhiniromocana sūtra.* The phrase in the Sanskrit is connected with the four *abhisaṃdhis* (types of "entangled" or "indirect" speech), cited in the *Mahāvyutpatti* (nos. 1671–75). Understanding such speech, the bodhisattva is able to comprehend the true meaning of the Dharma whether that meaning is expressed in direct or indirect fashion.

Now it should be understood that there are five kinds of actions *(karma)* concomitant with those five kinds of benefits. Namely, it should be understood that the action that goes along with the benefit of a peaceful mind is dwelling in the present life in the supreme station of happiness, i.e., that station of the bodhisattva familiar with praxis *(prayoga)* that leads to Enlightenment and destroys the physical and mental weariness of exertion.

It should be understood that the action for the bodhisattva that goes along with the benefit of possessing unimpeded knowledge in all the sciences is the maturation of all the Buddhadharmas, and that the action going along with the benefit of being unwearied by saṃsāra is the maturation of beings.

It should be understood that the action going along with understanding all the speech with "veiled intention" is that of removing the doubts that have arisen among the candidates *(vineya),* of holding them together, and of upholding the rule of Dharma *(dharmanetrya)* for a long time, by recognizing, exposing, and dispelling the fictitious resemblances to the True Dharma *(saddharma)* that cause the Teaching to disappear. And lastly, it should be understood that the action for the bodhisattva that goes along with the benefit of not depending on others and so not being led astray is his victory over all the heretical arguments by others, his steadfast striving, and his not falling away from his vow.

Concomitant with the five benefits attained by the bodhisattva, thus matured, are five actions or activities *(karmas).* As can be seen, these actions are enjoined upon the bodhisattva, as they serve to benefit not only him/herself but all other sentient beings as well. Hence the five are referred to as "bodhisattva duties" *(karaṇīyas).*

Accordingly, whatever the bodhisattva duty *(karaṇīya)* of the bodhisattva may be, all that is encompassed by these five actions going along with the benefits. Again, what is that duty? It consists of undefiled personal happiness, maturing the Buddhadharmas, maturing the beings, upholding the True Dharma, and defeating opposing theories, by one whose striving is fierce and whose vow does not waver.

With regard to all the foregoing, it should be understood that of the four sorts of knowledge of reality, the first two are inferior *(hīna),* the third is middling *(madhya),* but the fourth is the best *(uttama).*

Here ends the Chapter on Knowing Reality, being the fourth [chapter] in the first division *(yogasthāna)* of the *Bodhisattvabhūmi.*

The Chapter on Knowing Reality

(Running Translation)

[I]

What is knowledge of reality? Concisely, there are two sorts (1) that sort which consists of [knowing] the noumenal aspect *(yathāvadbhāvikatā)* of dharmas, or the true state of dharmas as they are in themselves *(bhūtatā);* and (2) that sort which consists of [knowing] the phenomenal aspect *(yāvadbhāvikatā)* of dharmas, as they are in totality *(sarvatā)*. In short, knowledge of reality should be understood as [knowledge of] "dharmas as they are, and as they are in totality."

Further, knowledge of reality may be given a fourfold analysis, as follows:

(1) what is universally accepted by ordinary beings;
(2) what is universally accepted by reason, or logic;
(3) that which is the sphere of cognitive activity *(jñānagocara)* completely purified of the obscurations of defilement *(kleśāvaraṇa);* and
(4) that which is the sphere of cognitive activity completely purified of obscurations to the knowable *(jñeyāvaraṇa)*.

Of these four, the first may be defined as follows: The shared opinion of all worldly beings—because their minds are involved with and proceed according to signs *(saṃketa)* and conventions *(saṃvṛti),* out of habit *(saṃstava)*—with respect to any "given thing" *(vastu),* is like so: "Earth is earth alone, and not fire." And as with earth, just so fire, water, wind, forms, sounds, smells, tastes, tactiles, food, drink, conveyance, clothes, ornaments, utensils, incense, garlands, ointments, dance, song, music, illumination, sexual intercourse, fields, shops, household objects, happiness, and suffering are viewed accordingly. "This is suffering, not happiness." "This is happiness, not suffering." In short, "This is this, and not that." And likewise, "This is this, and not any other."

Whatever given thing is taken hold of and becomes established for all ordinary beings owing merely to their own discursive thought *(vikalpa),* by means of associations *(saṃjña)* arising one after another in the sphere of foregone conclusions, without having been pondered, without having been weighed and measured, and without having been investigated, that is said to be the reality which is universally accepted by ordinary beings, or which is established by worldly consent.

What is that reality universally accepted by reason *(yukti)*? It is that which is known from the personal eloquence of those at the stage of being governed by reason, who are learned in the meaning of logical principles, and who have intelligence, reasoning power, and skill in investigation. Also, it is that knowledge arising in ordinary beings which is based on the authority of those engaged in investigation, namely, the proofs *(pramāṇa)* of the logicians: direct perception, inference, and the testimony of trustworthy persons. That is the sphere of well-analyzed knowledge wherein the knowable given thing is proven and established by demonstration-and-proof reason. That is said to be the reality which is universally accepted by reason.

What is the reality which is the sphere of cognitive activity completely purified of the obscurations of defilement? It is that domain and sphere of cognitive activity attained by putting an end to the outflows *(āsrava),* which is the "putting an end to the outflows" of all the śrāvakas and pratyekabuddhas, as well as that mundane knowledge which puts an end to the outflows at some future time. That reality is said to be the sphere of cognitive activity that is completely purified of the obscurations of defilement. When knowledge becomes purified of the obscurations of defilement, i.e., of those three mental supports [the three defilements], one dwells in nonobscuration. Therefore, it is called reality which is the sphere of cognitive activity completely purified of the obscurations of defilement.

Moreover, what is that reality? The Four Noble Truths, namely: (1) suffering, (2) its origin, (3) its cessation, and (4) the path leading to its cessation. It is that knowledge which arises in those having clear comprehension who, after thorough investigation, arrive at the understanding of these Four Noble Truths. Further, it is the understanding of those truths on the part of those śrāvakas and pratyekabuddhas who have apprehended that there are only aggregates *(skandha-mātra)* [in what is commonly assumed to be a person] and who have not apprehended a self *(ātman)* as a separate entity apart from the aggregates. By means of insight *(prajñā)* properly applied to the arising and passing away of all dependently arisen *(pratītyasamutpanna)*, conditioned states, clear vision *(darśana)* arises from the repetition of the view that "apart from the aggregates there is no 'person'."

What is the reality which is the sphere of cognitive activity completely purified of the obscurations to the knowable? That which prevents knowledge of a knowable is said to be an "obscuration." Whatever sphere of cognitive activity is completely freed from all obscurations to the knowable, just that should be understood to be the domain and sphere of cognitive activity completely purified of the obscurations to the knowable.

Again, what is that? It is the domain and the sphere of cognitive activity that belongs to the Buddha-Bhagavans and bodhisattvas who, having penetrated the non-self of dharmas *(dharmanairātmya),* and having realized, because of that pure understanding, the inexpressible nature *(nirabhilāpya-svabhāvatā)* of all dharmas, know the sameness *(sama)* of the essential nature of verbal designation *(prajñaptivāda)* and the nondiscursive knowable *(nirvikalpa-jñeya).* That is the supreme Suchness *(tathatā),* there being none higher, which is at the extreme limit of the knowable and for which all analyses of the dharmas are accomplished, and which they do not surpass.

Furthermore, it should be understood that the correctly determined *(vyavasthānataḥ)* characteristic of reality is its not-two *(advaya)* nature, or constitution *(prabhāvitaṃ).* The two are said to be "being" *(bhāva)* and "nonbeing" *(abhāva).*

With regard to those two, "being" is whatever is determined to have essential nature solely by virtue of verbal designation *(prajñaptivāda svabhāva),* and as such is clung to by the worldly for a long time. For ordinary beings, this [notion of being] is the root of all discursive thought and proliferation *(prapañca),* whether "form," "feeling," "ideation," "motivation," or "perception"; "eye," "ear," "nose," "tongue," "body," or "mind"; "earth," "water," "fire," or "wind"; "form," "sound," "smell," "taste," or "contact"; "skillful," "unskillful," or "indeterminate" acts; "birth" or "passing away" or "dependent arising"; "past," "future," or "present"; "compounded" or "uncompounded"; "This is a world, and beyond is a world," "There are both the sun and moon," and whatever is "seen," "heard," "believed," or "perceived"; what is "attained or striven for," what is "adumbrated" or "thought with signs" by the mind; even up to "Nirvāṇa." Everything in this category has a nature established by verbal designation only. This is said [by ordinary beings] to be "being."

With regard to those two, "nonbeing" is when the base of the verbal designation "form," and so on up to "Nirvāṇa," is absent or noncharacterizable; when the basis of verbal designation, with recourse to which verbal designation operates, is insubstantial, nonascertainable, nonexistent, or nonpresent in any way whatsoever. This is said to be "nonbeing."

Moreover, the given thing, comprised of dharma characteristics, that is completely freed from both "being" and "nonbeing"—i.e., from the "being" and "nonbeing" described above—is "not-two." Now, what is not-two, just that is said to be the incomparable Middle Path *(madhyamā pratipad)* which avoids the two extremes; and concerning that reality *(tattve)* the knowledge *(jñānam)* of all the Buddha-Bhagavans should be understood to be exceedingly pure. Further, it should be understood that that knowledge for the bodhisattvas constitutes the Path of Instruction *(śikṣa-mārga)*.

That insight is the bodhisattva's great means *(mahān upāya)* for reaching the Incomparable Perfect Enlightenment. And why? Because of the bodhisattva's firm conviction in voidness *(śūnyatādhimokṣa)*, practicing in these and those births and circling in saṃsāra for the sake of thoroughly ripening the Buddhadharmas for himself and other sentient beings, he comes to know saṃsāra as it really is. And moreover, he does not weary his mind with the aspects of impermanence and so forth which pertain to that saṃsāra. Should he not experience the true nature of saṃsāra, he would be unable, owing to all the defilements—of lust, hatred, delusion, and so forth—to render his mind equable; and not being equable, his defiled mind, circling in saṃsāra, would mature neither the Buddhadharmas nor the sentient beings.

Again, if he should weary his mind with the aspects of

saṃsāra, impermanence, and so forth, being thus [wearied] that bodhisattva would very quickly enter Parinirvāṇa. But the bodhisattva thus entering very quickly into Parinirvāṇa would mature neither the Buddhadharmas nor the sentient beings. Again, how would he become awakened to the Incomparable Perfect Enlightenment?

On account of his firm conviction in voidness, that bodhisattva, continuously applying himself, is neither frightened by Nirvāṇa nor does he strive toward Nirvāṇa. If that bodhisattva should be frightened by Nirvāṇa, he would not store up his equipment for Nirvāṇa hereafter; but rather, not seeing the benefits which lie in Nirvāṇa, owing to fear of it, that bodhisattva would give up the faith and conviction which sees the excellent qualities in that.

On the other hand, if that bodhisattva should frequently fix [his or her mind] zealously on Parinirvāṇa, he would speedily enter Parinirvāṇa. But as a result of quickly entering Parinirvāṇa, he would mature neither the Buddhadharmas nor the sentient beings.

In summary, whoever does not thoroughly experience saṃsāra as it really is circles in saṃsāra with a defiled mind. And whoever is wearied in mind by saṃsāra quickly enters Nirvāṇa. Whoever possesses a mind of fear with respect to Nirvāṇa does not store up equipment for it. And whoever fixes [his mind] zealously on Nirvāṇa quickly enters Parinirvāṇa. But it should be understood that these are not the bodhisattva's means for attaining Incomparable Perfect Enlightenment.

Again, whoever thoroughly experiences saṃsāra as it really is circles in saṃsāra with an undefiled mind. And whoever has a mind which is unwearied by the aspects of impermanence and so forth of saṃsāra, that one does not quickly enter Nirvāṇa. And whoever has a mind which is unfrightened by Nirvāṇa stores up equipment for it, and though seeing the good qualities and benefits in Nirvāṇa still does not exceedingly long for it, and so does not quickly enter Nirvāṇa. This is the bodhisattva's great means for attaining the Incomparable Perfect Enlightenment. And this means is well grounded in that firm conviction in supreme voidness. Therefore for the bodhisattva who has well taken hold of the Path of Instruction, cultivating conviction in supreme voidness is said to be the "Great Means" for reaching the knowledge of the Tathāgata.

Now you should know that that bodhisattva, because of his long-time engagement with the knowledge of dharma-selflessness, having understood the inexpressibility of all dharmas as they really are, does not at all imagine any dharma; otherwise he would not [truly] grasp "given thing only" as precisely "Suchness only." It does not occur to him, "This is the given thing only, and this other, the Suchness only." In clear understanding the bodhisattva courses, and coursing in this supreme understanding with insight into Suchness, he sees all dharmas as they really are, i.e., as being absolutely the same. And seeing everywhere sameness, his mind likewise, he attains to supreme equanimity.

Taking recourse in that equanimity, while greatly applying himself toward skill in all the sciences, that bodhisattva does not turn away from his goal because of fatigue, or because of any suffering. Unwearied in body and unwearied in mind, he quickly achieves skillfulness in those [sciences], and he reaches the stage of attaining the great power of mindfulness. He is not puffed up by virtue of his skill, nor does he have a teacher's closed-fistedness toward others. Not only does his mind not shrink from any skills, but also, with enthusiasm, he proceeds without hindrance. Practicing with steadfast mental armor:

to the extent that circling in saṃsāra he experiences diverse sufferings, to that extent he generates enthusiasm toward Incomparable Perfect Enlightenment;

to the extent that he experiences diverse bodies, to that extent he lacks pride toward any sentient being;

to the extent that he experiences diverse acquaintances[?], to that extent when associated with others seeking brawls and disputes, who are garrulous, have great and lesser defilements, and who practice unbridled and mistaken ways, as he experiences those ones, even to greater measure his mind stays in equanimity;

and to the extent that he grows in virtue, to that extent his goodness is unabated.

He does not seek to know from others nor does he seek gain or reverence [for himself]. These and numerous other benefits of the same category, i.e., the Wings of Enlightenment dharmas and all things consistent with Enlightenment, accrue for the bodhisattva who has that knowledge [of dharma-selflessness] as his excellent basis. Therefore, whoever sets out to attain Enlightenment, whoever will attain it, and those who do attain it, all these have as their basis that very same knowledge—not another knowledge, whether superior or inferior.

Having thus entered upon the practical application of the method without proliferation, the bodhisattva has many benefits: he rightly engages in thoroughly ripening the Buddhadharmas for himself, and for others, in thoroughly ripening the Dharma of the Three Vehicles. Moreover, thus rightly engaged, he is without craving for possessions or even for his own body.

He trains himself in noncraving so that he is able to give to sentient beings his possessions and even his own body. For the sake of sentient beings alone is he restrained, and well restrained, in body and speech. He trains himself in restraint so that he naturally takes no pleasure in sin, and so that he becomes wholesome and good by nature. He is forbearing toward all injury and wrongdoing on the part of others. He trains himself in forbearance so that he has little anger and so that he does no injury to others.

He becomes skillful and expert in all the sciences in order to dispell the doubts of sentient beings and to manage to assist them, and for himself, to embrace the cause of omniscience *(sarvajñānatā)*. His mind abides within, equipoised. And he trains himself in the fixing of his mind, so as to completely purify the Four Sublime Abodes (*caturbrāhmavihāra*), and to sport in the Five Supernormal Faculties (*pañcabhijñā*) in order to perform his duty toward all sentient beings, and in order to clear away all the fatigue that arose from his exertions to become expert. And he becomes wise, knowing the Supreme Reality *(paramatattvajñā)*. He trains himself to know the Supreme Reality, so that in the future he will himself, in the Great Vehicle, enter Parinirvāṇa.

You should know that the bodhisattva thus rightly engaged carefully attends all virtuous beings with worship and reverence. And all unvirtuous beings he carefully attends with a mind of sympathy and a mind of supreme compassion.

Insofar as he can and has the strength, he is engaged in dispersing their faults. He carefully attends all harmful beings with a mind of love. And insofar as he can and has the strength, being himself without trickery and without deceit, he works for their benefit and happiness, to eliminate the hostile consciousness of those who do evil because of their faults of expectation and practice. Unto helpful beings, after showing gratitude, he carefully attends them in return with more than equal helpfulness. And he fulfills their pious aspirations as much as he can and has the strength. Even when he is unable, not having been asked, he displays respectful endeavor toward these and those duties to be done. Never once does he reject duty. How should the notion occur to him, "I, being incapable, do not wish to do this"? This, and other actions of the same category, should be understood as the right procedure for the bodhisattva who, having taken up the way of nonproliferation, is well based in knowledge of Supreme Reality.

[II]

Now by what philosophical reasoning is the inexpressible character (*nirabhilāpya*) of all dharmas to be understood? As follows: Whatever is a designation for the individual characteristics of the dharmas, for example, "form" or "feeling" or the other personality aggregates, or, as before explained, even up to "Nirvāṇa," that should be understood to be only a designation. It is neither the essential nature *(svabhāva)* of that dharma, nor is it wholly other than that. That [essential nature] is neither the sphere of speech nor the object of speech; nor is it altogether different from these. That being the case, the essential nature of dharmas is not found in the way in which it is expressed. But further, neither is absolutely nothing found. Again, the essential nature is absent and yet not absolutely absent. One might ask: "How is it found?" It is found by avoiding grasping both the view which affirms the existence of what is nonexistent and the view which denies existence altogether. Moreover, one should understand that only the sphere of cognitive activity which is completely freed of discursive thought is the domain of knowledge of the supreme essential nature of all dharmas.

Again, if with regard to any dharma or any given thing it is assumed that it becomes just like its expression, then those dharmas and that given thing would be that expression itself. But if that were the case, then for a single dharma and a single given thing there would be very many kinds of essential nature. And why? It is like this: to a single dharma and to a single given thing, various men will attach many different designations by virtue of numerous expressions of various kinds. That dharma and that given thing ought to have identity with, be made up of, and have the essential nature of some one verbal designation, but not of the other remaining verbal designations. But there being no fixed determination, which of the very many kinds of verbal designation would hold as the correct one? Therefore, the use of any and all verbal designations, however complete or incomplete, for any and all given things does *not* mean that the latter are identical to, made up of, or receive essential nature through those verbal designations.

Now, to view it in another way, suppose the dharmas themselves, of form and so forth as previously expounded, should become the essential nature of their verbal designations. If this were the case, then, first there would be just the given thing alone, i.e., completely disassociated from names, and only afterward would there be the desire to attach to that given thing a verbal designation. But this would mean that before a verbal designation was attached, at the time just prior to attaching the designation, that very dharma and that very given thing would be without essential nature. But if there were no essential nature, there would be no given thing at all; and hence, a designation would not be called for. And since no verbal designation would be attached, the essential nature of the dharma and of the given thing could not be proved.

Again, suppose that just prior to the attaching of a verbal designation, that dharma and that given thing should be identical with the designation. This being the case, even without the verbal designation "form," the idea of form would occur whenever there was a dharma with the name "form," and whenever there was a given thing with the name "form." But such does not occur.

Now, through employing reasoning like this, one should understand that the essential nature of all dharmas is inexpressible, i.e., completely beyond the reach of expression. And one should understand that just as with regard to form, so with feelings, etc., as previously expounded, even up to Nirvāṇa itself.

It should be understood that these two views have fallen away from our Dharma-Vinaya: (1) that one which clings to affirming the existence of what are nonexistent individual characteristics, having essential nature only through verbal designations for a given thing, form, etc., or for the dharmas form and so forth; and also (2) that one which, with respect to a given thing *(vastu)*, denies the foundation for the sign of verbal designation, and the basis for the sign of verbal designation, which exists in an ultimate sense owing to its inexpressible essence, saying "absolutely everything is nonexistent."

The faults which result from affirming the existence of what is nonexistent have been examined, laid out, clarified and illumined immediately above. Because of these faults which arise from affirming the existence of nonexistents with respect to the given thing of form, etc., one should understand that view as having fallen away from our Dharma-Vinaya.

Likewise, denying the bare given thing, which is a universal denial *(sarvavaināśika),* has fallen away from our Dharma-Vinaya. I say, then: "Neither reality nor designation is known when the bare given thing, form and so forth, is denied. Both these views are incorrect."

Thus, if the aggregates of form exist, then the designation "person" is valid. But if they do not, the designation "person" is groundless. Attaching a verbal designation to the dharmas, form, etc., and to the bare given thing of form, etc., is valid when they are existent *(sat).* When they are not existent, the attaching of a verbal designation is groundless. And again, if there is no given thing present to be designated then since there is no foundation, there is also no designation.

Therefore, certain persons who have heard the abstruse sūtra passages associated with the Mahāyāna and associated with profound voidness, and that evince only an indirect meaning *(ābhiprāyikārtha),* do not understand the meaning of the teaching as it really is *(yathābhūta).* Those ones, imagining it superficially *(ayoniśa),* thus have views posited merely by logic, without cogency, and speak as follows: "All this reality is just designation only. And whoever sees accordingly, that one sees rightly." According to those, the given thing itself, which is the foundation for designation, is lacking. But if this were so, no designations would occur at all! How should reality, then, come to be solely designation?

Accordingly, they deny both these two, reality as well as designation. One should understand that the denial of both reality and designation is the position of the chief nihilist *(pradhāna nāstika).* Because his views are like this, the nihilist is not to be spoken with and not to be associated with by those intelligent ones *(vijña)* who live the pure life *(brahmacārin)*. Such a one, i.e., the nihilist, brings disaster even unto himself, and worldly ones who follow his view also fall into misfortune. In connection with this, the Lord has declared: "Indeed, better it is for a being to have the view of a 'person' than for one to have wrongly conceptualized voidness." And why? Because men who have the view of a 'person' are deluded only with respect to a single knowable, but they do not deny all knowables. And not for that reason alone would they be born among hell-beings.

Nor should another bring disaster to the seeker of Dharma, the seeker of liberation from suffering, nor deceive him. Rather, he should establish him in righteousness *(dharma)* and in Truth *(satya)*, and he should not be lax concerning the points of instruction. Because of the nihilist's wrongly conceptualized voidness, he is confused with respect to the knowable given thing of dharmas to the point of denying all knowables; and on that account one does get born among hell-beings. The nihilist would bring disaster to the righteous man, the seeker of liberation from suffering, and he would become lax concerning the points of instruction. Therefore, denying the given thing as it really is, he has strayed far from our Dharma-Vinaya.

Again, how is voidness wrongly conceptualized? There are some śramaṇas, as well as brāhmaṇas, who do not agree *(necchati)* concerning "owing to what there is a void"; nor do they agree concerning "that which is void." But such formulations as these are evidence of what is said to be "voidness wrongly conceptualized." And why? Voidness is logical when one thing is void of another because of that [other's] absence and because of the presence of the void thing itself. But how and for what reason would the void come to be from universal absence [*sarva-abhāvāt,* i.e., from complete nonexistence]?

Hence, the conception of voidness these describe is not valid. And therefore, in this manner voidness is wrongly conceptualized.

Now, how is voidness rightly conceptualized? Wherever and in whatever place something is not, one rightly observes that [place] to be void of that [thing]. Moreover, whatever remains in that place one knows *(prajanati)* as it really is, that "here there is an existent." This is said to be engagement with voidness as it really is and without waywardness. For example, when a given thing, as indicated, is termed "form," etc., there is no dharma identical to the verbal designation "form" and so on. Hence, whenever a dharma is termed "form" etc., that given thing is void of identity with the verbal designation "form," etc. Then what remains in that place when a given thing is termed "form," etc.? As follows: just the basis *(āśraya)* of the verbal designation "form," etc. When one knows both those as they really are—namely, that there is just a given thing and there is just a designation for just a given thing—then he neither affirms the existence of what is nonexistent nor denies what is existent. He neither makes it in excess nor makes it in deficiency. He neither minimizes nor adds.

And when he knows Suchness, as it really is, with its inexpressible essential nature, as it really is, this is called "voidness rightly conceptualized," and called "well-discerned right insight." By this means, and others consistent with demonstration-and-proof reasoning, he will come to judge that the essential nature of all dharmas is inexpressible.

ON KNOWING REALITY: RUNNING TRANSLATION

[III]

Moreover, one should understand that all dharmas have an inexpressible essential nature from the scriptures *(āgama)* of a trustworthy person *(āpta)*. This very meaning was expressed by the Lord through an elucidating verse *(gāthābhigīta)* in the "Discourse on Transference in Phenomenal Life" *(Bhavasaṃkrāntisūtra)*:

Indeed, by whatsoever name whatsoever dharma is mentioned, that dharma is not found therein. For that is the true nature of all dharmas.

How does this verse elucidate our very meaning? When a dharma has the name "form" and so on, whatever the name be, i.e., "form," etc., by means of that name the dharmas are referred to with the names "form" etc., whether form or feeling and so on up to Nirvāṇa. But the dharmas having those names "form" etc. are themselves not identical with the designations "form," etc. Nor is there any dharma found outside of those that is identical to "form," etc. Again, for those dharmas having the names "form," etc., one should understand that what does exist there in the ultimate sense, with an inexpressible meaning, is the true mode *(dharmatā)* of essential nature. And it was spoken by the Lord in the discourse treating the categories of dharmas [the *Arthavargīya*]:

Whatever conventions there be among the worldly, all those the Muni does not take up. And verily not participating, how could he indulge, since he takes no pleasure in what is seen or heard?

ON KNOWING REALITY: RUNNING TRANSLATION

How does this verse elucidate our very meaning? Whatever be the designations, such as "form," etc., applied to a dharma of form, etc., those are said to be "conventions." He does not accept that dharmas are identical with those designations. In this respect, he does not accept those conventions. And why? Because his view is neither that of exaggeration *(samāropa)* nor of underestimation *(apavāda)*. Now because he does not have a wayward *(viparyāsa)* view, he is said to not participate. Thus not participating, how is he to indulge? Without that wayward view, he neither affirms nor denies that given thing; and not indulging, he rightly sees in the knowable what is to be seen of it. And what he hears spoken of the knowable was indeed heard of it. In regard to what is seen and heard, he neither originates nor increases craving. Not otherwise would he rid himself of the object of consciousness *(ālambana)* and dwell with equanimity; and having equanimity, he does not create desire *(kāntim)*.

And again, such was declared by the Lord in the discourse beginning with the story of the "Saṃtha Kātyāyana." In this account, the monk having the title "Saṃtha" meditates neither upon the base *(āyatana)* earth, water, fire, nor wind; neither upon the bases space, perception, or nothing-at-all, nor ideation nor nonideation; neither upon this world nor the other; neither upon the sun nor the moon; nor upon what is seen, heard, thought, perceived, obtained, striven for, inquired about, or concluded about by the mind. None of these does he employ as a meditative base. Now since he does not meditate upon the base earth, etc., nor all the rest, upon what does he meditate? Here, for the saṃtha monk, whatever the idea *(saṃjñā)* of "earth" regarding earth, that idea is lost *(vibhūtā)*. Whatever the idea of "water" with regard to water, and with regard to all the rest, that idea is lost. Thus this monk meditates, not using earth as a meditative base nor any of the others. Using none of them at all as a meditative base, he meditates. Therefore do all the gods along with Indra, along with the Īśānas, and along with Prajāpati, bow down near the monk thus meditating, saying,

> Salutations to this noble man. Salutations to the best of men. To you for whom there is nothing further to know, resorting to what will you meditate?

Again, how does this sūtra verse elucidate our very intent? For given things named "earth," etc., "earth" and so on are only nominal designations. For those given things named "earth," etc., the idea of them arises with exaggeration, or the idea of them arises with underestimation. The idea with "exaggeration" posits the essential nature of the given thing as consisting of that name; and the idea with "underestimation" posits the destruction of the ultimate basis of the given thing itself. When these two erroneous views are abandoned and eliminated, the idea of any meditative base is said to be "lost."

Therefore from the scriptures and also from the Tathāgata's supreme lineage of trustworthy successors, one should understand that all dharmas have an inexpressible essential nature. Now, since all dharmas have thus inexpressible essential nature, why is expression applicable at all? Verily, because without expression, the inexpressible true nature could not be told to others, nor heard by others. And if it were neither spoken nor heard, then the inexpressible essential nature could not become known. Therefore, expression is applicable for producing knowledge through hearing.

ON KNOWING REALITY: RUNNING TRANSLATION

[IV]

Precisely because that Suchness is not thoroughly known *(aparijñātatva),* the eight kinds of discursive thought *(vikalpa)* arise for immature beings *(bāla)* and operate so as to create the three bases *(trivastu),* which further produce the receptacle worlds *(bhājanaloka)* of all sentient beings. The eight are as follows: (1) discursive thought concerning essential nature; (2) discursive thought concerning particularity; (3) discursive thought concerning grasping whole shapes; (4) discursive thought concerning "I"; (5) discursive thought concerning "mine"; (6) discursive thought concerning the agreeable; (7) discursive thought concerning the disagreeable; and (8) discursive thought contrary to both these.

Further, these eight kinds of discursive thought create what three bases? The discursive thought concerning essential nature, the discursive thought concerning particularity, and the discursive thought concerning grasping whole shapes, these three engender the [perceivable] base which is named "form," etc., i.e., the base which serves as the foundation of discursive proliferation and as its mental support *(ālambana).* With that [perceivable] base as its foundation, discursive thought—saturated with words, ideas, and names and enveloped in words, ideas, and names—proliferates and ranges on that base in many ways.

Of these eight, the discursive thought concerning "I" and the discursive thought concerning "mine" engender the reifying view *(satkāyadṛṣṭi),* and the root of all other views, namely: the root of pride *(māna),* the root of egoism *(asmimāna),* and the root of all other self-centered views.

Among those eight, discursive thought concerning the

agreeable and the disagreeable, as well as discursive thought which is contrary to both these, engender, according to the circumstances, desire, hatred, or delusion *(rāgadveṣamoha)*. Thus do these eight kinds of discursive thought serve to manifest the three kinds of bases, namely: (1) the [perceivable] base which serves as the foundation of discursive thought and its proliferation; (2) the base of the reifying view, egoism, and pride; and (3) the base of lust, hatred, and delusion. With regard to those, when the [perceivable] base of discursive thought together with proliferation exist, then the reifying view and the "I am" pride have a support; and when the reifying view and the "I am" pride exist, then lust, hatred, and delusion have a support. Further, these three bases explain completely the manifold evolution of all the worlds [of saṃsāra].

1. Among those eight, what is discursive thought concerning essential nature? It is that discursive thought which designates "form," etc., when there is a given thing of form, etc. This is said to be discursive thought concerning essential nature.

2. What is discursive thought concerning particularity? It is that discursive thought which, when there is a given thing named "form," etc., thinks, "This has form," "This is formless," "This is shown," "This is not shown," "This has hindrance," "This is unhindered," "This is outflow," "This is not outflow," "This is compounded," "This is uncompounded," "virtuous," "unvirtuous," "indeterminate," "past," "future," "present"; and by way of immeasurable distinctions of the same category, whatever discursive thought is founded upon the discursive thought concerning essential nature, with the object of particularizing it, this is said to be discursive thought concerning particularity.

3. What is discursive thought concerning grasping whole

shapes? When there is a given thing named "form," etc., whatever operates to grasp whole shapes with respect to the multiple dharmas taken together, adding to given things nominal designations like "self," "life," and "sentient being"; and adding nominal designations like "house," "army," and "forest," "food," "drink," "conveyance," and "clothes," etc., this is said to be discursive thought concerning grasping whole shapes.

4. 5. What is discursive thought concerning "I" and "mine"? When a given thing has outflow, is graspable, and for a long time has been familiar, clung to *(abhiniviṣṭa)*, and thought of as "self" *(ātmata)*, or as "what belongs to self" *(ātmīyata)* so by intimacy with that errant way of conceptualizing, discursive thought wrongly takes the given thing, which has arisen dependently, as having been placed there by one's own view. This is said to be discursive thought concerning "I" and "mine."

6. What is discursive thought concerning the agreeable? It is that discursive thought which has as its mental support a given thing which is pleasant and captivating to the mind.

7. What is discursive thought concerning the disagreeable? It is that discursive thought which has as its mental support a given thing which is unpleasant and revolting to the mind.

8. What is discursive thought which is contrary to both the agreeable and the disagreeable? It is that discursive thought which has as its mental support a given thing which is neither pleasant nor unpleasant, neither captivating nor revolting to the mind.

And this whole process is composed of two elements only: discursive thought, and the given thing which then becomes the mental support of discursive thought and the foundation of discursive thought. It should be understood that these two are mutually caused *(anyonya hetuka)* and without beginning in time. A previous discursive thought is the cause which generates a present given thing which, in turn, becomes the mental support of discursive thought. And again, the generated given thing which is the present mental support for discursive thought is the cause which generates the future discursive thought, having that as its mental support.

Now, with respect to this, it is precisely from lack of understanding that the discursive thought of the present is the cause which generates the given thing in the future—and that this given thing in turn becomes the mental support of discursive thought in the future—that there is the inevitable *(niyata)* generation of discursive thought in the future, having that thing as its foundation and as its basis.

But now how does thorough knowledge *(parijñāna)* of discursive thought arise? It arises by means of the four thorough investigations *(paryeṣaṇās)* and by means of the four kinds of knowing precisely and in detail *(yathābhūtaparijñānas)*. What are the four thorough investigations? They are the investigation of the name, the investigation of the given thing, the investigation of the designations for essential nature, and the investigation of the designations for particularity.

With respect to these, investigation of the name means that the bodhisattva sees with regard to a name that it is just a name. Likewise, with regard to a given thing, seeing that it is just a given thing is the investigation of the given thing. With respect to designations for essential nature, clearly seeing those as just designations for essential nature is the investigation of designations for essential nature; and with regard to designations for particularity, seeing those as just designations for particularity is the investigation of designations for particularity. He sees names and given things as having distinct characteristics *(bhinna lakṣaṇa)* and as having connected characteristics *(anuśliṣṭa lakṣaṇa);* and he realizes *(pratividhyati)* that designations for essential nature and designations for particularity are based upon the connected characteristics of the name and the given thing.

What are the four kinds of knowing precisely, in detail? They are knowing in detail the investigated name, the investigated given thing, the designations for essential nature, and designations for particularity—knowing all these precisely, in detail.

What is knowing precisely, in detail the investigated name? You should know that the bodhisattva, having investigated name as name only, knows that name just as it really is; to wit, he determines that "This name is the linguistic unit for a given thing"; likewise "the linguistic unit for conceptualizing, the linguistic unit for viewing, and the linguistic unit for attributing *(upacāra).*" If, for a given thing ordinarily conceived of as form, etc., a name "form," is not decided upon, no one would thus conceive that given thing as form; and not conceiving it, he would not exaggerate or cling to it. And not clinging to it, he could not express it. Thus he knows it precisely, in detail. This is said to be knowing the investigated name precisely, in detail.

What is knowing precisely, in detail, the investigated given thing? For any given thing, the bodhisattva, having investigated it as given thing only, sees that that given thing, while conceived of as "form," etc., and while associated with all the expressions [for it], is in itself inexpressible. This is the second knowing in detail, namely, knowing precisely, in detail the investigated given thing.

What is knowing precisely, in detail the investigated designations for essential nature? It is that knowing whereby the bodhisattva, with regard to a given thing conceived of as "form," etc., after having investigated its designations for essential nature as designations only, knows and well knows in detail that in designations relating to that given thing there is only the mere semblance of essential nature, and that in truth essential nature is lacking there. For him, seeing that "essential nature" as but a magical creation, a reflected image, an echo, a hallucination, the moon's reflection in the waters, a dream and an illusion, he knows that this semblance is not made up of that essential nature. This is the third knowing precisely, in detail, which is the sphere of most profound knowledge *(sugambhīrārtha gocara)*.

What is knowing precisely, in detail, the investigated designations for particularity? It is that knowing whereby the bodhisattva, after having investigated the designations for particularity as designations only attached to the given things called "form," etc., sees designations for particularity as having a not-two meaning. The given thing is neither completely present nor completely absent [neither existent nor nonexistent]. It is not present, since it is not "perfected" *(pariniṣpannatva)* owing to its expressible self. And it is not altogether absent, since in fact it is determined to have an inexpressible essence. Thus from the stance of absolute truth *(paramārthasatya)*, it is not formed *(rūpī)*, yet from the stance of relative truth *(saṃvṛitisatya)* it is not formless, since form is attributed to it. As with presence and absence, and formed and formless, just so is whatever is shown or not shown, etc. All the enumerations of designations for particularity should be understood in just this same manner. He [the bodhisattva] knows in detail as having a not-two meaning, whatever be the designations for particularity. This is knowing precisely, in detail the investigated designations for particularity.

Now it should be understood that those eight kinds of errant *(mithyā)* discursive thought which belong to immature beings and which engender the three bases and cause the continual return to the world, operate through weakness of, and nonengagement with, these four kinds of knowing precisely, in detail. Moreover, from errant discursive thought defilement arises; from defilement, circling in saṃsāra; from circling in saṃsāra, the consequences of saṃsāra, i.e., the sufferings of birth, old age, disease, and death.

But whenever the bodhisattva resorts to the four kinds of knowing precisely, in detail, he knows the eight kinds of discursive thought. And because of his right knowledge, in his lifetime *(dṛṣṭe dharme)* there is no generation, now or in the future, of a given thing associated with proliferation which could serve as a mental support and as a foundation for discursive thought. And because discursive thought does not arise, there is no generation in the future of a given thing having that as its support. Thus for him that discursive thought, along with the given thing, ceases *(nirodha)*. This should be understood as the cessation of all proliferation.

Therefore, one should understand the complete cessation of proliferation as the bodhisattva's "Parinirvāṇa of the Great Vehicle." Because of the complete purity of his knowledge, now the sphere of the most splendid knowledge of reality, in this lifetime that bodhisattva attains the mastery of power everywhere *(sarvatra vaśitāprāpti);* for example, he attains the mastery of multiform magical creation *(nirmāṇa)* owing to the magical power *(ṛddhi)* of creating; of multiform transformation *(pariṇāma)* owing to the magical power of transformation; of knowledge of all knowables; of remaining in the world as long as he wishes, and of departing from the world at his pleasure, without hindrance.

Thus, that one, with that mastery of power, is best of and incomparable among all beings. And you should understand that this bodhisattva has five superior benefits *(anuśaṃsā)* which control in all circumstances, namely: (1) he attains supreme peace of mind, because he attains the tranquil stations *(vihārapraśāntatayā)*, and not by reason of pacifying defilement; (2) his knowledge and vision with respect to all the sciences are unimpeded, extremely pure, and perfectly clear; (3) he is unwearied by his circling in saṃsāra for the sake of beings; (4) he understands all the speech with "veiled intention" *(saṃdhāya vacanāni)* of the Tathāgatas; and (5) because he is self-reliant, not depending on others, he is not led away from his zealous devotion *(adhimukti)* to the Great Vehicle.

Now it should be understood that there are five kinds of actions *(karma)* concomitant with those five kinds of benefits. Namely, it should be understood that the action that goes along with the benefit of a peaceful mind is dwelling in the present life in the supreme station of happiness, i.e., that station of the bodhisattva familiar with praxis *(prayoga)* that leads to Enlightenment and destroys the physical and mental weariness of exertion.

It should be understood that the action for the bodhisattva that goes along with the benefit of possessing unimpeded knowledge in all the sciences is the maturation of all the Buddhadharmas, and that the action going along with the benefit of being unwearied by saṃsāra is the maturation of beings.

It should be understood that the action going along with understanding all the speech with "veiled intention" is that of removing the doubts that have arisen among the candidates *(vineya)*, of holding them together, and of upholding the rule of Dharma *(dharmanetryā)* for a long time, by recognizing, exposing, and dispelling the fictitious resemblances to the True Dharma *(saddharma)* that cause the Teaching to disappear. And lastly, it should be understood that the action for the bodhisattva that goes along with the benefit of not depending on others and so not being led astray is his victory over all heretical arguments by others, his steadfast striving, and his not falling away from his vow.

Accordingly, whatever the bodhisattva duty *(karaṇīya)* of the bodhisattva may be, all that is encompassed by these five actions going along with the benefits. Again, what is that duty? It consists of undefiled personal happiness, maturing the Buddhadharmas, maturing the beings, upholding the True Dharma, and defeating opposing theories, by one whose striving is fierce and whose vow does not waver.

With regard to all the foregoing, it should be understood that of the four sorts of knowledge of reality, the first two are inferior *(hīna),* the third is middling *(madhya),* but the fourth is the best *(uttama).*

Here ends the Chapter on Knowing Reality, being the fourth [chapter] in the first division *(yogasthāna)* of the *Bodhisattvabhūmi.*

Glossary

All the terms listed here are found in the main body of this work. However, for the reader who may wish a brief summation of meanings in a readily available form, the following is provided. All terms are listed initially in Sanskrit. Tibetan equivalents are given in parentheses, immediately following. Proper names are given only in Sanskrit unless marked otherwise.

ābhiprāyika (dgoṅs pa can)
Veiled; indirect. Appearing especially in connection with *artha* (meaning) or *vacanan* (speech), this term characterizes what is "cloaked" or "veiled." Thus, having veiled or indirect meaning; not readily accessible to superficial investigation.

abhiṣeka (dbaṅ bskur)
Tantric initiation. Literally, "sprinkling [water] from above," the term originally referred to the coronation ceremony of an Indian monarch. Later, it came to symbolize the attainment of Buddhahood and to name the rite marking entrance into the esoteric doctrine of Buddhism. The water in the case of esoteric initiations represents the five kinds of wisdom of the Buddha.

Acinta
Tāranātha's *History* gives the spelling *acintya,* meaning "inconceivable" or "surpassing thought." S. C. Dass makes the term synonymous with *Ajānta,* the famed Buddhist monastic institution in South India. Asaṅga journeys to this "town" just prior to his miraculous meeting with Lord Maitreya.

advaya (gñis su med pa)
Literally, "not-two." "Nondual" is a common rendering but is inappropriate in the context of this work. See the text for fuller explication.

ālambana (dmigs pa)
The object, or mental support, of consciousness. Often used in

reference to meditation where it connotes the meditative object or visualization.

anātman (bdag med pa)

A kernel doctrine of Buddhist philosophy, claiming the absence of a "self" in truth; the denial of the existence of an abiding, self-existent principle in either the so-called "self" or in "things."

anuśaṃsa (phan yon)

Here, the benefits (numbering five) which accrue for the bodhisattva who has attained "nondiscursive knowledge," and which are said to "control in all circumstances."

anyonya hetuka (gcig gi rgyu las gcig byuṅ ba yin pa)

Mutual production, or genesis in dependence each on the other. Literally, "from the cause of the one, the other arises." The concept of mutual production and dependence is fundamental to Asaṅga's explication here wherein it is shown that discursive thought occasions the given thing, while the presence of the given thing generates discursive thought. Likewise, there being things, names arise, and vice-versa. This process of mutual dependence is further characterized as being "beginningless."

apavada (skur pa 'debs pa)

Denial or rejection. The term used to characterize the "extreme" view of underestimation. With *samāropa* (exaggeration), the term forms a technical pair indicating the two errant views which have "fallen away" from the Middle Path.

arhat (dgra bcom pa)

The "ideal" of early Buddhist Hīnayāna practice. This title is given to one who has "conquered" *(hata)* his "enemies" *(ari)*, where "enemies" refers to the three primary defilements *(kleśas)*: hatred, greed, and delusion.

artha (don)

Knowledge; meaning; linguistic unit. The usual rendering for this term is "meaning." However, in the context of the present chapter it is often used as a synonym for *jñāna*, or knowledge. In order, then, to render the major, epistemological, thrust of the chapter, it is rendered here as "knowledge" or "knowing." In addition, it is sometimes treated as that which causes knowledge or which "creates meaning" (Tib. *don byed)*. In reference to specific written "signs" for things, it is also appropriately rendered "linguistic unit."

GLOSSARY

ārya ('phags pa)

A title of great respect meaning "noble." This title is often applied to Asaṅga.

āsrava (zag pa)

Literally "outflow"; that which issues forth or causes swelling. In Asaṅga's *Bodhisattvabhūmi,* the *āsravas* are identified with the primary *kleśas* (defilements) of greed, hatred, and delusion.

ātman (bdag pa)

The term denoting the supposed "self."

Avalokiteśvara

Literally, the "Lord who looks [lovingly] down [upon the suffering beings]." The name is used to refer especially to the compassionate aspect of Buddhahood. Historically, Avalokiteśvara was a disciple and contemporary of Gautama Buddha who made the "Great Vow" to liberate all sentient beings from suffering. Some centuries later, a cult arose in India around the worship of Avalokiteśvara as a deity in his own right, complete with full iconographic detailing.

avaraṇa (sgrib pa)

A covering or veil which hinders a clear view of reality.

āyatana (skye mched)

The twelve "factors" of consciousness, comprised of the six sense organs (including mind as the sixth) and their respective sense objects. These are the fundamental elements of Buddhist epistemological analysis.

bhāva (yod pa)

Literally, "being"; the chapter treats the term as synonymous with *vastu* (Tib. *dṅos po),* i.e., "any existent thing," or any compounded, perceptible entity.

bhūmi (sa)

Literally, earth or ground; the term also connotes degree, step, level, or stage. The name of the work entitled the *Bodhisattvabhūmi* may thus be translated as "The Stages of One Intent on Enlightenment."

bhūtatā (yaṅ dag pa ñid)

The true state of things. The noumenal aspect of reality. Reality in itself.

bodhi (byaṅ chub)

Enlightenment; the term used to characterize the *summum bonum* of Mahāyāna Buddhist practice.

GLOSSARY

bodhisattva (byaṅ chub sem dpa')
One who is intent on (attaining) enlightenment.

Buddhadharmas (saṅs rgyas kyi chos)
The various types of knowledge, attainments, methods, and teachings associated with a Buddha, or fully enlightened being.

caitya (chos rten)
A reliquary mound figuring prominently in early Buddhist architecture.

citta (sems; yid)
A term employed variously to connote mind, consciousness, or thought itself.

cittamātra (sems tsam)
The term is usually rendered incorrectly as "mind-only" with an absolutist connotation. As a proper noun, it is used to refer to the school of Mahāyāna Buddhist thought founded by Maitreya and Asaṅga. A later, alternate, name is Vijñānavāda.

dharma (chos)
As is well known to students of Buddhism, this term is extremely difficult to translate (and it has been deemed best to leave it untranslated in the body of the present work in order to avoid confusion and unnecessary complication). It is used variously, but in philosophical contexts generally refers to any existent reality or phenomenon—however fleeting in terms of temporal duration. Dharmas in such contexts may be said to be phenomena or events which are both generated and experienced by consciousness. Moreover, the term is usually reserved for phenomena which are compounded, and hence dependent, existents.

Dharma (chos)
The Holy Teaching of the Buddha. Buddhist Doctrine.

dharmadhātu (chos kyi dbyiṅs)
Literally, the "realm of [all] dharmas," this term is used to characterize the totality of existents and hence to demarcate the limits of reality. It is sometimes employed as a title for ultimate reality.

Dharmapāla
Indian Buddhist doctor whose commentaries, notably on Vasubandhu's *Viṃśatikā* and *Triṃśikā,* served as the foundation for the great synthesis of Yogācārin thought translated by Hsüang-tsang as the *Ch'eng wei Shih lun,* i.e., the *Vijñaptimātratāsiddhi.*

GLOSSARY

Dharma-Vinaya (chos 'dul ba)
Vinaya refers to the second of the so-called "baskets" *(piṭakas)* of the Buddhist canon, namely, that one dealing specifically with the code of monastic discipline. Therefore, Asaṅga's use of the compound term *Dharma-Vinaya* is intended to delimit what properly constitutes true Buddhist doctrine and practice.

dhyāna (bsam gtan)
Meditative absorption. The term refers specifically to one of the four successive stages of complete concentration accompanied by (1) joy and reflection; (2) joy and the absence of reflection; (3) being freed of joy, and equable; and (4) supreme equanimity.

dṛṣṭi (lta ba)
View. Used especially of a philosophical position.

duḥkha (sdug bsṅal)
Usually rendered "suffering," the term refers to all forms of discomfort or dis-ease. It is the chief mark of saṃsāric existence.

dveṣa (źe sdaṅ)
Hatred. One of the three primary *kleśas* or defilements (in the compound: desire, hatred, and delusion).

Gambhīrapakṣa
The Indian king who became Asaṅga's royal patron.

dGe lugs pa (Tib.)
Literally, "Virtuous one," the name refers to the school of Tibetan Buddhism founded by the fourteenth-century teacher Tsoṅ-kha-pa.

gocara (spyod yul)
Sphere of activity. In conjunction with *jñāna* (knowledge), the area or place of operation of the cognitive process.

Guṇaprabha
A commentator. Though noted primarily for his commentary on the *śīla* chapter of the *Bodhisattvabhūmi,* Guṇaprabha wrote an exegesis of the entire work, called the *Bodhisattvabhūmivṛtti.*

Hīnayāna (theg pa dman)
That "vehicle" of Buddhist practice which stresses teachings aimed at "individual" *(hīna)* liberation from suffering.

Hsüan-tsang
Famed Chinese translator of numerous Buddhist philosophical treatises. Responsible for introducing into China the "later" tradition of Yogācāra thought, he is mentioned here especially in

connection with his translating work on the *Ch'eng wei Shih lun*, or *Vijñaptimātratāsiddhi*.

jñāna (śes pa)

Knowledge, both mundane and supramundane. (The Tibetan sometimes reserves *ye śes* for that type of supramundane knowledge possessed by the Buddhas.)

jñāna-gocara (śes pa'i spyod yul)

Rendered here as the "sphere of cognitive activity," the phrase connotes both the place or location of knowledge (i.e., *gocara* or *yul)* and the knowledge itself. The term is descriptive in nature, suggesting the image of consciousness enveloping its "object" (the knowable entity) in such a way that there is the dissolution of both the subject (i.e., the "knowing" consciousness) and the object (where the knowable entity = *gocara,* or the "area of operation" of consciousness).

jñeya (śes bya)

Any knowable entity or phenomena. Literally, that which generates knowledge. Hence, the phenomenon which serves as a basis of knowledge.

bKa' gdams pa (Tib.)

The school of Tibetan Buddhism founded by the Indian pandit Atiśa while journeying in Tibet to teach the Dharma. The school was further developed by the disciple, Brom, and later became the reformed *dGe lugs pa* sect under the great Tsoṅ-kha-pa.

kalyāṇamitra (dge ba'i bśes gñen)

Literally, the "best or the most splendid friend" *(mitra)*, the term is used as a title with which one refers to one's *guru* or "root" teacher.

karaṇīya (bya ba)

Literally, "what is to be done," i.e., duty. Here, referring to the five duties enjoined on bodhisattvas who have attained to "non-discursive knowledge."

karma (las)

From the Sanskrit verb root *kṛ*, "to do or make"; the noun means "action." In Buddhism, the term refers especially to the law of cause and effect, i.e., to the principle that every action produces some result.

kleśa (ñon moṅs pa)

From the Sanskrit verb root *kliṣ*, meaning "to be afflicted or stricken by"; the noun in Buddhism refers especially to the painful emotions of hatred, greed, and delusion; defilements.

Kukkuṭapāda

The name of the mountain which served as the place of solitary retreat for Asaṅga's twelve arduous years of meditation.

lakṣaṇa (mtshan ñid)

A mark or sign. In Buddhist philosophy, a characteristic or distinguishing feature. An attribute (of a substance). In the context of the present chapter, the term refers to those "individual characteristics" which have existence solely by virtue of designations.

mahān upāya (thabs chen po)

Literally, the "great" *(mahān)* "means" *(upāya)* of a bodhisattva for accomplishing his/her end of liberating all sentient beings. *Upāya* may be rendered also as "method" or "expedient device."

Mahāyāna (theg pa chen po)

Literally, the "Great Vehicle." The name given to the "later" phase of Buddhist thought wherein the concepts of compassion and virtuous, selfless activity chiefly characterize practice, while a proper understanding of the doctrine of *śūnyatā* (voidness) predominates in terms of theory.

Mahīśāsaka

The name of the sect to which Asaṅga belonged before "entering the Mahāyāna."

māna (ṅa rgyal)

Pride; egocentricity. The Tibetan rendered literally is "[treating the] 'I' as king."

Maitreya

The reputed historical teacher of Asaṅga. The name also refers to Asaṅga's tutelary deity, Lord Maitreya, who represents the Buddha's aspect as "love" *(maitri)*.

mithyā (log pa)

Errant. Incorrect. Used especially with reference to formulations of logic.

moha (gti mug)

Delusion. The "fog" of ignorance.

Nāgārjuna

Renowned doctor of Mahāyāna Buddhist philosophy, most noted for his explication of the doctrine of *śūnyatā* in the work *Mūlamadhyāmakakārikā*.

GLOSSARY

nairātmya (bdag med pa)

Non-self. The descriptive term in Buddhist philosophy used to assert the absence of an abiding "self" or "essence" in the entity to which it is applied.

nāma (miṅ)

Name. A nominal designation, assignation, or imputation. Also, the whole process of imputation.

rNam thar (Tib.)

An abbreviation for *rnam par thar pa,* i.e., "complete liberation." The term is used to refer to a genre of literature which records "complete liberation [life stories]," or "sacred biography." Most notable among *rNam thar* are the biographies of the Indian Buddhist yogis, the Mahāsiddhas.

nirmāṇa (sprul pa)

Magically created appearance. Used especially with reference to the bodies of enlightened beings.

Nirvāṇa (mya ṅan las 'das pa)

The state which represents the goal of Hīnayāna practice.

nirvikalpa (rnam par mi rtog pa)

Literally, "no discursive thought," the term describes that state of cognizing reality which is totally freed of the distortions of discursive thought. In association with *jñāna* (knowledge), then, the term characterizes the bodhisattva's direct perception of reality as it really is. According to the chapter, this is a synonym for the highest and best knowledge of reality.

Paramārtha

The great Indian sage who is noted especially for having imported many Buddhist texts into China. He is reputed to have translated the texts of both Asaṅga and Vasubandhu into Chinese following his arrival in China around 548 A.D. Especially valuable is his *Life of Vasubandhu,* and we learn much of the life of Asaṅga from it.

paramārtha-satya (don dam bden pa)

According to Mahāyāna philosophy, the truth *(satya)* which is in accord with the ultimate or most supreme *(parama),* meaning *(artha).* Hence, "absolute truth."

pāramitā (pha rol tu phyin pa)

Transcendent action. The term refers to the six transcendent actions of the bodhisattva, with respect to giving, moral discipline, patience, energy, meditation, and insight.

paratantra (gźan gyi dbaṅ)

The name given to the second of the "three natures." The "dependency" nature; literally, "getting its power from another." In Asaṅga's system, this "dependency" nature is represented by the *vastu* (i.e., the given thing which serves as a base of imputation).

parikalpita (kun brtags pa)

Imaginary. Mentally fabricated. The name given to the first of the "three natures" according to Asaṅga's explication. In the context of the chapter, this imaginary nature is represented by names and designations.

pariniṣpanna (yoṅs su grub pa)

"Perfected." The term used to characterize the third of the "three natures" *(svabhāvas)* according to Asaṅga's system. It corresponds to the "absolute truth" of the "two truths" doctrine, and describes the ultimate cognition of reality, freed of all distorting influences.

paryeṣaṇa (yoṅs su tshol ba)

Translated here as "thorough investigation," the term refers specifically to the four searches—of name, given thing, designations for essential nature, and designations for particularity—which may be conducted by śrāvakas and pratyekabuddhas as well as bodhisattvas.

paṭalam (le 'u)

A chapter, or division of a book.

Piṇḍola

One of the Hīnayāna teachers of Asaṅga, referred to in Paramārtha's account as having attained the rank of an *arhat.*

piṭaka (sde snod)

Literally, "basket," the term is used to refer to any of the three "collections" of the Buddhist scriptures (i.e., *sūtra,* or discourses, *vinaya,* monastic rules, and *abhidharma,* commentaries focusing on subtler points of philosophical and psychological explication).

prajñā (śes rab)

Insight. The highest form of knowledge, direct and penetrative, yielding an unhindered and unadulterated view of reality. That type of knowledge possessed by all Buddhas.

GLOSSARY

prajñāpāramitā (śes rab kyi pha rol tu phyin pa)
The transcendent action (or practice) of ultimate insight.

prajñapti (gdags pa)
Designation. Also, the compound phenomenon of mental image together with name. As "mental imputation" on to a base of imputation (here, *vastu*), this term forms an essential ingredient in Asaṅga's explication here.

prajñaptivāda ('dogs pa'i tshig)
Verbal designation. Also, the view which holds the real existence of names (or designations).

pramāṇa (tshad ma)
The sources or "proofs" of knowledge which, according to Asaṅga, are three in number: direct perception, inference, and trustworthy scripture or testimony.

prapañca (spros pa)
Proliferation. Here, especially proliferation of discursive thought *(vikalpa)*, engendering the seemingly endless procession of names and concomitant things *(vastus)*. On account of *prapañca* there is the continuous "running on" of thought (i.e., names, discriminations, judgments, etc.) such that reality is never experienced directly as it really is, freed of distorting superimpositions. Therefore, Asaṅga encourages the bodhisattva who seeks true knowledge of reality to "engage the method without proliferation."

Prasannaśīlā
Asaṅga's mother. Her name is recorded as Prakāśaśīlā in some accounts.

pratītyasamutpāda (rten ciṅ 'brel par 'byuṅ pa)
One of the quintessential doctrines of Buddhist philosophy, the term is a descriptive phrase which characterizes that type of origin or "arising" *(utpada)* which occurs "together with" *(sam)* or is occasioned by (i.e., is dependent upon) the occasion of some other phenomenon. The term, especially in the context of the chapter, shares affinity with the phrase *anyonya hetuka*, that is, "mutual production."

pratyekabuddha (raṅ saṅs rgyas)
Literally, "enlightenment for oneself alone," the term refers to a category of Buddhist practitioners who apparently train for and realize enlightenment in isolation.

GLOSSARY

prayoga (sbyor ba)
Here, the integration of theory and practice exercised by the bodhisattva.

pudgala (gaṅ zag)
The term used to designate a "person" or "individual." It is often a synonym for *ātman,* or "self." The literal rendering of the Tibetan is "whatever is swollen" or "puffed up."

rāga ('dod chags)
Desire. First member of the threefold grouping of primary *kleśas,* i.e., desire, hatred, and delusion.

ṛddhi (rdsu 'phrul)
Magical power.

saddharma (dam pa'i chos)
The True Doctrine.

Sāgaramegha
Author of a commentary on the whole of Asaṅga's *Yogācārabhūmiśāstra,* Sāgaramegha is mentioned here especially in connection with his exegesis of the *Bodhisattvabhūmi* section of the work, entitled the *Yogācāryabhūmau bodhisattvabhūmi vyākhyā.*

samādhi (tiṅ ṅe 'dsin)
The term used in meditation theory to denote complete integration and absorption.

samāropa (sgro 'dogs pa)
The "extreme" view of affirmation. The view which exaggerates or overestimates the thing in question. *Samāropa* and its opposite *(apavada,* "denial") form a technical pair characterizing errant views divergent from the Buddhist Middle Path.

samatā (mtshuṅs pa ñid)
The key term of the chapter, employed by Asaṅga to denote the "sameness" of essential nature for all phenomena—whether of the "self" or of "things," generally. *Samatā* is a more positive synonym for *śūnyatā* ("voidness" or "emptiness"), though it points to the same characterization of reality. The essential nature of all phenomena is, absolutely speaking, the same *(sama),* i.e., void *(śūnya)* of an abiding self, or of self-existence.

saṃjñā ('du śes)
One of the five personality aggregates, or *skandhas,* the term is variously rendered as "motivations" or "ideations." In the context

of the chapter it is clear that it is associated with the naming faculty and with mental associations in general.

saṃketa (brda)

A sign, written or verbal. Here, especially linguistic signs. Words. Conventions of language.

saṃsāra ('khor ba)

Literally, "continuous going"; the term refers to that whole round of mental and physical existence marked by lack of rest, and by a constant sense of uneasiness, pain, and discomfort.

saṃstava ('dris pa)

Habit. The term refers both to particular views as well as to actions which are performed automatically, without discipline or prior investigation.

saṃvṛti (kun rdzob)

In combination with *satya* ("truth") the term is rendered "relative" (as opposed to "absolute" truth). Relative; worldly. Here also, "conventions" of language, written and verbal.

Saṅghabhadra

The renowned Buddhist master of Kashmir who instructed Vasubandhu in the philosophical traditions of early Buddhism.

sarvatā (tham cad ñid)

Literally, "totality," the term refers here to the whole of phenomenal existence. The phenomenal aspect of reality as contrasted with the noumenal *(bhūtatā)* aspect.

satkāyadṛṣṭi ('jig tshogs la lta ba)

The reifying view. That view which posits a concrete, self-centered reality, based on the notions of "I" and "mine."

satya (bden pa)

Truth. Literally, what is in accordance with reality *(sat)*.

śīla (tshul khrims)

Moral virtue and discipline. Virtuous behavior as well as deportment.

skandha (phuṅ po)

Literally, "shoulder" in Sanskrit and "heap" in Tibetan, the term refers figuratively to the "bearer of the burden [of the ego]." It is used in Buddhist philosophy and psychology to denote the five personality aggregates or psychophysical elements commonly thought of as a "self" or "person."

GLOSSARY

śrāvaka (ñon thos)

Literally, a "hearer"; one who heard the Buddha's discourses as they were preached. The term is used primarily to refer to monks of the Hīnayāna tradition.

Sthiramati

Disciple of Vasubandhu. Sthiramati's commentaries on works by Asaṅga and Vasubandhu are invaluable as aids to a proper understanding of "early" Yogācāra thought.

śūnyatā (stoṅ pa ñid)

Voidness. The characterization of the ultimate state of things, i.e., as void of an abiding "self" or essential nature.

svabhāva (ṅo bo ñid)

Literally, "own-being" or "self-existence," the term is here translated as "essential nature." Also, "aspect" or "nature," especially in connection with the threefold epistemological schema expounded by Asaṅga.

bstan 'gyur (Tib.)

The title given to the complete collections of the Buddhist commentarial tradition in Tibetan which, together with the translated discourses *(sūtra)* of the Buddha, comprise the Tibetan Buddhist Canon.

Tathāgata (de bźin gśegs pa)

An epithet of a Buddha, meaning literally "he who has 'thus gone' or has 'thus come,' " with reference to the Way or Path to Enlightenment.

tathatā (de bźin ñid)

Literally, "thusness" or "suchness," the term is a synonym for *śūnyatā* and *samatā* and characterizes the ultimate state of reality, freed of all determinate description.

tattva (de kho na [*ñid*])

Literally, "thatness," the term is used in the chapter to refer to reality itself, in its ultimate state, devoid of all characterization.

triyāna (theg pa gsum)

Literally, the "Three Vehicles" of Buddhism: (1) the Śrāvaka Vehicle, or way of the "hearers"; (2) the Pratyekabuddha Vehicle, or path of those intent on salvation for themselves alone; and (3) the Bodhisattva Vehicle, carrier of those intent upon enlightenment for the sake of all beings.

Tsoṅ-kha-pa (Tib.)

The renowned fourteenth-century Tibetan Buddhist teacher who founded the reformed *dGe lugs pa* sect and authored voluminous works on Buddhist doctrine and practice. Especially noted for the *Lam rim chen mo,* or the "Great [treatise] on the Graded Path [to Enlightenment]."

Tuṣita

Literally, "wholly satisfied," the term names the Buddhist "heaven" or realm which serves as the abode for all bodhisattvas just prior to their entrance into the phenomenal world. Hence, the place from which all future Buddhas issue.

vaśita (mṅa 'ba; dbaṅ)

Powers; especially that group of ten powers which accrue to a bodhisattva of the eighth stage.

vastu (dṅos po)

The given thing at hand. The object upon which cognitive attention is focused. Any perceivable entity serving as a base for cognition/imputation. Proper understanding of this term is essential for correct comprehension of Asaṅga's entire explication. Translated here as the "given thing," *vastu* is properly the *base of imputation.* On to this base, various names are attached (as well as aberrant judgments and other forms of mental imputation, such as the assertion of "externality").

In accordance with Asaṅga's "three nature" theory, the *vastu* is the key representative of the *paratantra* (i.e., dependency) nature. While the naming process is considered totally imaginary *(parikalpita* nature), being false, aberrant, and imparting no truth, nevertheless imputation occurs only in relation to some base of imputation (i.e., a *vastu)* which must exist in some way (even if that mode of existence is imperfect). Correct understanding of both the nature of imputation and of the base of imputation yields insight which is, according to Asaṅga's terminology, "perfected," i.e., *pariniṣpanna.*

Vasubandhu

The younger half-brother of Asaṅga, whom he converted to the Mahāyāna. Vasubandhu later became the chief expositor and popularizer of Asaṅga's system.

vidyasthāna (rig pa'i gnas)

Literally, "stations of knowledge," the term refers to the five branches of traditional Buddhist learning, i.e., in philosophy, logic, grammar, medicine, and arts and crafts.

vijñapti (rnam par rig pa)

Conceptualization. The term describes ordinary cognition, wherein the perception of a given thing is distorted by superimpositions, judgments, and conceptualizations of all sorts. In Asaṅga's system the term is often a synonym for *vijñāna (rnam par śes pa).*

vikalpa (rnam par rtog pa)

Discursive, undisciplined thought of all kinds, whether names, images, judgments, or whatever. According to Asaṅga's explication, discursive thought generates both names and things, i.e., both imputations and bases of imputation, respectively. Hence, owing to discursive thought, there is the presence of both the *parikalpita* nature (names) as well as the *paratantra* nature (i.e., things, here *vastus*). Neither of these two natures is "perfected" *(pariniṣpanna),* however: hence the chapter's great emphasis on the attainment of *nirvikalpa-jñāna,* or "nondiscursive knowledge." The eight kinds of *vikalpa,* in their Sanskrit and Tibetan equivalents, are as follows: (1) *svabhāvavikalpa* = *ṅo bo ñid du rnam par rtog pa;* (2) *viśeṣavikalpa* = *bye brag tu rnam par rtog pa;* (3) *piṇḍagrāhavikalpa* = *ril por 'dzin pa'i rnam par rtog pa;* (4) *ahamiti vikalpa* = *bdag go snam pa'i rnam par rtog pa;* (5) *mameti vikalpa* = *bdag gi snam pa'i rnam par rtog pa;* (6) *priyavikalpa* = *sdug par rnam par rtog pa;* (7) *apriyavikalpa* = *mi sdug par rnam par rtog pa;* (8) *tadubhayaviparīta vikalpa* = *de ga ni las bzlog pa'i rnam par rtog pa.*

viparyāsa (phyin ci log)

Here, rendered "wayward view," the term refers in Buddhist literature to four specific misconceptions, namely: (1) taking as permanent what is really impermanent; (2) taking as self-possessing what is without self; (3) taking as pure what is impure; and (4) taking as pleasant what is really painful.

yathābhūta (yaṅ dag pa ji lta ba bźin du)

A descriptive term used to characterize the ultimate state of reality, freed of all superimpositions; rendered here by the phrase "as it really is," i.e., in-itself.

yoga (rnal 'byor)

From the Sanskrit root, *yuj,* "to join together," the term generally refers to practices—both physical and mental—aimed at bringing about a state of holistic integration.

Yogācāra

The name of the school of Buddhist explication founded in the fourth century A.D. by Maitreya and Asaṅga. Later also referred to as the *Vijñānavāda*.

yukti (rigs pa)

That type of reasoning which employs logical principles and analysis.

Selected Bibliography

Works of Asaṅga

Abhidharmasamuccaya. *(a)* Pralhad Pradhan, ed. *Abhidharma Samuccaya of Asaṅga.* Santiniketan: Visva-Bharati, 1950. *(b)* Walpola Rahula, tr. *Le compendium de la super-doctrine (Abhidharmasamuccaya) d'Asaṅga.* Paris: École française d'Extrême-Orient, 1971.

Bodhisattvabhūmi. *(a)* Nalinaksha Dutt, ed. *Bodhisattvabhūmi.* Tibetan Sanskrit Works Series, no. 7. Patna: K. P. Jayaswal Research Institute, 1966. *(b)* U. Wogihara, ed. *Bodhisattvabhūmi* (2 vols.). Tokyo, 1930–36.

Mahāyānasaṃgraha. Étienne Lamotte, ed. (Tibetan ed.) and tr. *La Somme du Grand Véhicule d'Asaṅga (Mahāyānasaṃgraha).* Louvain: Muséon, 1938–39.

Tattvārtha-paṭala. Sanskrit editions: *(a)* N. Dutt, ed. *Bodhisattvabhūmi,* Tibetan Sanskrit Works Series, vol. 7. Patna: K. P. Jayaswal Research Institute, 1966. Devanāgari text, pp. 25–39. *(b)* U. Wogihara, ed. *Bodhisattvabhūmi,* vol. 1, Tokyo, 1930. Romanized text, pp. 37–57. Tibetan edition: *(c) Tibetan Tripiṭaka,* Peking edition (the *PTT);* D. T. Suzuki, ed., rpt. ed., Kyoto: Otani University, 1957. Vol. 110 *(bstan-'gyur, sems-tsam, shi,* folio sides 24b–37b), pp. 142–47. *(d)* Guṇaprabha's commentary on the chapter, entitled the *Bodhisattvabhūmivṛtti,* in *PTT,* vol. 112 *(bstan 'gyur, sems-tsam Yi,* folio sides 196b–203b), pp. 9–12. *(e)* Sāgaramegha's commentary, the *Yogācāryabhūmau bodhisattvabhūmi vyākhyā, PTT,* vol. 112 *(bstan-'gyur, sems-tsam Ri,* folio sides 63b–91b), pp. 69–80.

Tattvārtha-viniścaya saṃgrahaṇī. Tibetan edition only. *PTT,* vol. 111 *(bstan-'gyur, sems-tsam Hi,* folio sides 19b–29b), pp. 72–76.

Vajracchedikaprajñāpāramitāsūtraśāstrakārikā. Giuseppe Tucci, ed. and tr. *The Triśatikāyāḥ Prajñāpāramitāyāḥ Kārikāsaptatiḥ by Asaṅga* in *Minor Buddhist Texts,* Part I. Rome: *Serie Orientale Roma,* vol. 9 (1956), pp. 1–128.

Yogācārabhūmiśāstra. V. Bhattacharya, ed. *The Yogācārabhūmi of Acārya Asaṅga: Part I* (bhūmis 1–5 of the *Bahubhūmikavastu).* Calcutta: University of Calcutta, 1957.

Other Sanskrit and Tibetan Works

Abhidharmakośa. *(a)* Louis de La Vallée Poussin, ed. and tr. *L'Abhidharmakośa de Vasubandhu.* 6 vols. Louvain: Muséon, 1923–31. *(b)* Louis de La Vallée Poussin, *L'Abhidharmakośa de Vasubandhu: Introduction, Fragment des Kārikās, Index, Additions.* Paris: Geuthner, 1931.

Abhisamayālaṅkāra. *(a)* E. Obermiller and Th. Stcherbatsky, eds. *Abhisamayālaṃkāraprajñāpāramitopadeśaśāstra.* Bibliotheca Buddhica, no. 23. Leningrad, 1929. *(b)* Edward Conze, tr. *Abhisamayālaṅkāra.* Rome: Serie Orientale Roma, no. 6, 1954.

Aṣṭasahāśrika Prajñāpāramitā. *(a)* Edward Conze, ed. *Aṣṭasahaśrika Prajñāpāramitā.* Calcutta: Asiatic Society, 1958. *(b)* Edward Conze, tr. *The Aṣṭasahaśrika Prajñāpāramitā; Perfection of Wisdom in Eight Thousand Ślokas.* Bibliotheca Indica, 1970. Reprinted as *The Perfection of Wisdom in Eight Thousand Lines.* Bolinas, Calif.: Four Seasons Foundation, 1973.

Bhavasaṃkrāntisūtra. N. A. Sastri, ed. and tr. *Bhavasaṃkrāntisūtra.* Adyar Library, 1938.

Buddhacarita. *(a)* E. H. Johnston, ed. *Buddhacarita.* Punjab University Publications, no. 31. Calcutta: Punjab University, 1936. *(b)* E. H. Johnston. tr. *Acts of the Buddha.* Punjab University Publications, no. 32. Calcutta: Punjab University, 1936.

Bu-ston. *Chos-'byung.* E. Obermiller, tr. *History of Buddhism by Buston.* 2 vols. Heidelberg, 1931.

Daśabhūmikasūtra *(a)* J. Rahder, ed. *Daśabhūmikasūtra et Bodhisat-*

tvabhūmi: Chapitres Vihāra et Bhūmi. Paris and Louvain, 1926. *(b)* Megumu Honda and J. Rahder, trs. *Annotated Translation of the Daśabhūmika-Sūtra.* Śatapiṭaka Series, no. 74. New Delhi: International Academy of Indian Culture, 1968.

Laṅkāvatārasūtra. *(a)* Bunyiu Nanjio, ed. *Laṅkāvatāra-sūtra.* Tokyo, 1923. *(b)* D. T. Suzuki, tr. *Laṅkāvatārasūtra.* London, 1932. *(c)* D. T. Suzuki. *Studies in the Laṅkāvatāra Sūtra.* London: George Routledge and Sons, 1930.

Madhyāntavibhāga. *(a)* Ramchandra Pandeya, ed. *Madhyānta-Vibhāga-Śāstra.* Delhi: Motilal Banarsidass, 1971. *(b)* Chandradhar Sharma, ed. *Ārya Maitreya's Madhyānta-Vibhāga-Shāstra.* Jabalpur: Shrimate Shanti Sharma, 1963. *(c)* S. Yamaguchi, ed. *Madhyāntavibhaṅga.* 2 vols. Nagoya, 1934. *(d)* Th. Stcherbatsky, tr. *The Madhyānta-vibhaṅga.* Bibliotheca Buddhica, no. 30. Leningrad, 1936. *(e)* Paul O'Brien, tr. "A Chapter on Reality from the Madhyāntavibhāgaçāstra," in *Monumenta Nipponica.* Vols. IX and X. Tokyo: Sophia University, 1953–54. *(f)* Gadjin M. Nagao, ed. *Madhyāntavibhāga-Bhāṣya.* Tokyo: Suzuki Research Foundation, 1964.

Mahāyānasūtrālaṅkāra. *(a)* S. Bagchi, ed. *Mahāyāna-Sūtrālaṅkāra of Asaṅga.* Buddhist Sanskrit Texts, no. 13. Darbhanga: Mithila Institute of Post-Graduate Studies and Research in Sanskrit Learning, 1970. *(b)* Sylvain Lévi, ed. and tr. *Mahāyāna-Sūtrālaṃkāra.* Paris: Champion, 1907 and 1911. *(c)* Gadjin M. Nagao. *Mahāyāna-Sūtrālaṃkāra, Index to the (Lévi edition).* Parts I and II. Tokyo: Nippon Gakujutsu Shinko-Kai, 1958 and 1961.

Mahāvyutpatti. Sakaki, ed. *Mahāvyutpatti,* 2 vols. Kyoto: 1916–25 and 1928.

Nāgārjuna. *Mūlamadhyamakakārikā.* *(a)* Louis de La Vallée Poussin, ed. *Mūlamadhyamakakārikās (Mādhyamikasūtras) de Nāgārjuna avec la Prasannāpada Commentaire de Candrakīrti.* St. Petersburg: Bibliotheca Buddhica, 1903–13. *(b)* Kenneth Inada, ed. and tr. *(Nāgārjuna's) Mūlamadhyamakakārikā.* Tokyo: Hokuseido Press, 1970.

mKhas grub rje. Ferdinand Lessing and Alex Wayman, eds. and trs. *mKhas grub rje's Fundamentals of the Buddhist Tantras.* The Hague: Mouton, 1968.

Ratnagotravibhāga. *(a)* E. Johnston, Skt. ed. Patna: Bihar Research Society, 1950. *(b)* E. Obermiller, tr. (from Tibetan). "The Sublime

Science of the Great Vehicle to Salvation," *Acta Orientalia*, no. 9 (1931). *(c)* Jikido Takasaki. *A Study on the Ratnagotravibhāga (Uttaratantra)*. Rome: Serie Orientale Roma, no. 33, 1966.

Saddharmapuṇḍarīka sūtra. (a) H. Kern, tr. *The Saddharma-Puṇḍarīka or The Lotus of the True Law.* Sacred Books of the East, no. 21. Oxford, Clarendon Press, 1909. *(b)* Leon Hurvitz, tr. *Scripture of the Lotus Blossom of the Fine Dharma (The Lotus Sūtra).* Translations from the Oriental Classics series. New York: Columbia University Press, 1976.

Saṃdhinirmocanasūtra. Étienne Lamotte, ed. and tr. (from Tibetan). *Saṃdhinirmocana Sūtra: L'explication des Mystères.* Université de Louvain Publication, no. 34. Louvain and Paris: Université de Louvain, 1935.

Saṃyutta-nikāya. (a) L. Feer, ed. Pāli Text Society. 5 vols. 1884–98 (rpt., London: Pāli Text Society, 1960). *(b)* C. A. Rhys Davids and F. L. Woodward, trans. *Kindred Sayings.* Pāli Text Society, 1917–30.

Śrāvakabhūmi. Alex Wayman. *Analysis of the Śrāvakabhūmi Manuscript.* Berkeley: University of California Press, 1961.

Śrī-Mālā-sūtra. Alex and Hideko Wayman, trs. *The Lion's Roar of Queen Śrīmālā.* New York: Columbia University Press, 1974.

Sthiramati. *Madhyānta-vibhāga-ṭīka.* S. Yamaguchi, ed. *Madhyānta-vibhāga-ṭīka.* Tokyo: Suzuki Research Foundation, 1966.

Sutta-Nipāta. (a) Dines Anderson and Helmer Smith, eds. *Sutta-Nipāta.* Pāli Text Society. London: Oxford University Press, 1913. *(b)* M. Coomaraswamy, tr. *Sutta Nipāta.* London: Trübner, 1874.

Tāranātha. *History of Buddhism in India.* Translated from Tibetan by A. Chattopadhyaya and Lama Chimpa. Simla: Indian Institute of Advanced Study, 1970.

Tsoṅ-kha-pa. *Sṅags rim chen mo.* Jeffrey Hopkins, ed. and tr. *Tantra in Tibet: The Great Exposition of Secret Mantra by Tsoṅ-ka-pa.* The Wisdom of Tibet Series, no. 3. London: George Allen and Unwin, 1977.

Vijñaptimātratāsiddhi. (a) Louis de La Vallée Poussin, ed. and tr. *Vijñaptimātratāsiddhi—La Siddhi de Hiuan-tsang,* 2 vols. Paris, 1925–28. *(b)* La Vallée Poussin. *Vijñaptimātratāsiddhi; La Siddhi de Hiuan tsang, Index to.* Paris: 1948. *(c)* Clarence Hamilton, tr. *Wei Shih Er Shih Lun: The Treatise in Twenty Stanzas on Representation-Only.* New Haven: American Oriental Society, 1938.

Vimalakīrtinirdeśasūtra. Robert A. Thurman, ed. and tr. *The Holy Teaching of Vimalakīrti: A Mahāyāna Scripture*. University Park: The Pennsylvania State University Press, 1976.
Visuddhimagga. Bhikkhu Ñyaṇamoli, tr. *(Buddhaghoṣa's) The Path of Purification (Visuddhimagga)*. Vols. I and II. Berkeley: Shambala, 1976.
Yogācārabhūmi of Saṅgharakṣa. Paul Demiéville, tr. "La *Yogācārabhūmi* de Saṅgharakṣa," *Bulletin de l'école française d'éxtrême Orient*, no. 44 (Hanoi, 1954).

Secondary Sources

Bapat, P. V., ed. *2500 Years of Buddhism*. New Delhi: Publications Division, Ministry of Information, 1956.
Bareau, André. *Les Sectes Bouddhiques du Petit Véhicule*. Saigon, 1955.
Beyer, Stephan. *The Cult of Tārā: Magic and Ritual in Tibet*. Berkeley: University of California Press, 1973.
Bharati, Agehananda. *The Tantric Tradition*. London: Rider, 1965.
Bhattacharyya, Benoytosh. *An Introduction to Buddhist Esoterism*. Mysore: (Humphrey Milford) Oxford University Press, 1932.
Bhattacharyya, K. *Studies in Philosophy*. Vol. I. Calcutta: Progressive Publishers, 1956.
Bradley, F. H. *Appearance and Reality: A Metaphysical Essay*. Oxford: Oxford University Press, 1969.
Chatterjee, A. K. *The Yogācāra Idealism*. Varanasi: Banaras Hindu University Press, 1962.
Conze, Edward. *Buddhist Thought in India*. Ann Arbor: The University of Michigan Press, 1967.
—— *Buddhist Wisdom Books*. London: Allen and Unwin, 1958.
—— *Materials for a Dictionary of the Prajñāpāramitā Literature*. Tokyo: Suzuki Research Foundation, 1967.
—— "The Ontology of the Prajñā-Pāramitā." *Philosophy East and West*, 3, no. 2 (1953), 117–29.
—— *The Prajñāpāramitā Literature*. The Hague. Mouton, 1960.
—— "The Yogācārin Treatment of Prajñāpāramitā Texts." In *Proceedings of the 23rd Congress of Orientalists*. Cambridge, 1959, pp. 230–31.
Coomaraswamy, Ananda K. *Buddha and the Gospel of Buddhism*. Lon-

don: George G. Harrap and Company, 1916. Rpt., New York: Harper and Row (Torchbook edition), 1964.

Dasgupta, Shashi Bhushan. *An Introduction to Tantric Buddhism.* Calcutta: Calcutta University Press, 1958.

—— *Obscure Religious Cults.* Calcutta: K. L. Mukhopadhyay, 1962.

Dasgupta, Surendranath. *Indian Idealism.* Cambridge: Cambridge University Press, 1969.

Dass, Sarat Chandra. *A Tibetan-English Dictionary.* Rev. ed. Delhi: Motilal Banarsidass, 1970.

Datta, D. M. *The Six Ways of Knowing: A Critical Study of the Advaita Theory of Knowledge.* Calcutta: University of Calcutta, 1972.

Dayal, Har. *The Bodhisattva Doctrine in Buddhist Sanskrit Literature.* London: Routledge and Kegan Paul, 1932.

Dutt, Nalinaksha. *Aspects of Mahāyāna Buddhism and Its Relation to Hīnayāna.* London: Luzac, 1930.

—— *Buddhist Sects in India.* Calcutta: K. L. Mukhopadhyay, 1970.

—— *Early Monastic Buddhism.* Calcutta: K. L. Mukhopadhyay. 1971.

Dutt, Sukumar. *Buddhist Monks and Monasteries of India.* London: George Allen and Unwin, 1962.

Edgerton, Franklin. *Buddhist Hybrid Sanskrit Dictionary.* Rpt., Delhi: Motilal Banarsidass, 1970.

Frauwallner, E. "On the Date of the Buddhist Master of the Law, Vasubandhu." *Serie Orientale Roma,* 3 (1951).

Govinda, Anagarika. *The Psychological Attitude of Early Buddhist Philosophy.* New York: Samuel Weiser, 1974.

Guenther, Herbert V. *The Tantric View of Life.* Boulder, Colo.: Shambala, 1976.

Guenther, Herbert V., and Leslie S. Kawamura. *Mind In Buddhist Psychology.* Emeryville, Calif.: Dharma Publishing, 1975.

Guenther, H. V., and Chögyam Trungpa. *The Dawn of Tantra.* Berkeley: Shambala, 1975.

Hakeda, Yoshito S. *The Awakening of Faith.* New York: Columbia Univeristy Press, 1967.

Hamilton, Clarence H. *Buddhism, a Religion of Infinite Compassion: Selections from Buddhist Literature.* New York: Liberal Arts Press, 1952.

—— "K'uei Chi's Commentary on Wei-Shih-Er-Shih-Lun." *Journal of the American Oriental Society,* 53 (1933), 144–51.

Horner, I. B. *Women Under Primitive Buddhism.* London: Routledge and Kegan Paul, 1930. Rpt., Delhi: Motilal Banarsidass, 1975.

SELECTED BIBLIOGRAPHY

Jaini, Padmanabh. "Origin and Development of the Theory of Viprayuktasaṃskāras." *Bulletin of the School of Oriental and African Studies* (University of London), 23, part 3 (1959), 531–47.

Jayatilleke, K. N. *Early Buddhist Theory of Knowledge.* London: Allen and Unwin, 1963.

Kalupahana, David J. *Buddhist Philosophy: A Historical Analysis.* Honolulu: The University Press of Hawaii, 1976.

Keith, Arthur B. *Buddhist Philosophy in India and Ceylon.* Oxford: Clarendon Press, 1923.

Lamotte, Étienne. *Histoire du Bouddhisme Indien.* Louvain: Muséon, 1958.

MacDonell, Arthur. *A History of Sanskrit Literature.* New York: Appleton, 1900. Rpt., Delhi: Motilal Banarsidass, 1971.

—— *India's Past: A Survey of Her Literatures, Religions, Languages, and Antiquities.* Oxford: Clarendon Press, 1927.

McGovern, W. M. *A Manual of Buddhist Philosophy.* New York: E. P. Dutton, 1923.

Mahāthera, Paravahera Vajirañāṇa. *Buddhist Meditation in Theory and Practice.* Colombo: M. D. Gunasena, 1962.

Majumdar, R. C. *Ancient India.* Delhi: Motilal Banarsidass, 1971.

Malalasekera, G. P. *Dictionary of Pāli Proper Names.* Indian Texts Series. 2 vols. London: Murray, 1937–38.

—— ed. *Encyclopaedia of Buddhism.* Vol. 1. Part I: A-Aca. Colombo, Ceylon: The Government Press, 1961.

Matilal, Bimal Krishna. "A Critique of Buddhist Idealism," in L. Cousins et al., eds., *Buddhist Studies in Honour of I. B. Horner.* Dordrecht, Holland: D. Reidel, 1974.

—— "Indian Theories of Knowledge and Truth" (review article), *Philosophy East and West,* 18, no. 4. (1968), 321–33.

—— *The Navya-Nyaya Doctrine of Negation.* Harvard Oriental Series, vol. 46. Cambridge: Harvard University Press, 1968.

Monier-Williams, Sir Monier. *A Sanskrit-English Dictionary.* Rpt., Oxford: Clarendon Press, 1964.

Murti, T. R. V. *The Central Philosophy of Buddhism.* London: Allen and Unwin, 1955.

Nagao, Gadjin. "President's Address" to the International Association of Buddhist Studies, First Conference, New York, September 15, 1978.

Nariman, J. K. *Literary History of Sanskrit Buddhism.* Delhi: Motilal Banarsidass, 1972.

SELECTED BIBLIOGRAPHY

Obermiller, E. *Analysis of the Abhisamayālaṃkāra*. Gaekwad Oriental Series, no. 27. Baroda: University of Baroda, 1933–39.

—— "A Study of the Twenty Aspects of Śūnyatā (Based on Haribhadra's Abhisamayālaṃkāraloka and the Pañcaviṃśatisahaśrikaprajñāpāramitāsūtra)," *Indian Historical Quarterly*, 9 (1933), 170–87.

—— "The Doctrine of Prajñāpāramitā as exposed in the Abhisamayālaṃkāra of Maitreya," *Acta Orientalia*, 11 (1932), 1–133.

—— "The Term Śūnyatā in its Different Interpretations," *Journal of Greater India Society*, 1 (1934), 105–17.

Potter, Karl. *Presuppositions of India's Philosophies*. Englewood Cliffs, N.J.: Prentice-Hall, 1963.

Rahula, Walpola. "Vijñaptimātratā Philosophy in the Yogācāra System and Some Wrong Notions," *The Middle Way: Journal of the Buddhist Society*, 47, no. 3 (1972).

—— *What the Buddha Taught*. New York: Grove Press, 1959.

Raju, P. T. *Idealistic Thought of India*. Cambridge: Harvard University Press, 1953.

Ramanan, K. Venkata. *Nāgārjuna's Philosophy*. Rutland, Vt.: Charles E. Tuttle, 1966.

Robinson, Richard H. *Early Mādhyamika in India and China*. Delhi: Motilal Banarsidass, 1976.

—— *The Buddhist Religion*. Belmont, Calif.: Dickenson, 1970.

Schmithausen, Lambert. "On the Problem of the Relation of Spiritual Practice and Philosophical Theory in Buddhism," in *German Scholars on India*. Contributions to Indian Studies, vol. II. Bombay: Nachiketa Publications, 1976.

Sharma, Dhirendra. *The Negative Dialectics of India*. Leiden: E. J. Brill, 1970.

Sopa, Geshe Lhundup, and Jeffrey Hopkins. *Practice and Theory of Tibetan Buddhism*. New York: Grove Press, 1976.

Speyer, J. S. tr. *Jātakamāla: Garland of Birth Stories*. Sacred Books of the Buddhists, no. I. London, 1895.

Stcherbatsky, Th. *Buddhist Logic*. 2 vols. New York: Dover, 1962.

—— *Soul Theory of the Buddhists*. Varanasi: Bharatiya Vidya Prakasan, 1970.

—— *The Central Conception of Buddhism*. Calcutta: Susil Gupta, 1932.

—— *The Conception of Buddhist Nirvāṇa*. Leningrad: Academy of Sciences of the USSR, 1927.

SELECTED BIBLIOGRAPHY

Strawson, P. F. *Individuals: An Essay in Descriptive Metaphysics.* London: Methuen, 1961.

Streng, Frederick J. *Emptiness: A Study in Religious Meaning.* New York: Abingdon Press, 1967.

Suzuki, D. T. *On Indian Mahāyāna Buddhism.* New York: Harper and Row, 1968.

—— *Outlines of Mahāyāna Buddhism.* New York: Schocken, 1963.

Swartz, Robert J., ed. *Perceiving, Sensing and Knowing.* New York: Doubleday, 1965.

Takakusu, Junjiro. *The Essentials of Buddhist Philosophy.* 1947. Rpt., Honolulu: University of Hawaii Press, 1956.

—— "The Life of Vasu-bandhu by Paramārtha (A.D. 499–569)," *T'oung Pao,* ser. II, 5 (1904), 269–96.

Thomas, Edward J. *The History of Buddhist Thought.* London: Routledge and Kegan Paul, 1951.

Tripathi, C. L. *The Problems of Knowledge in Yogācāra Buddhism.* Varanasi: Bharat-Bharati, 1972.

Thurman, Robert A. F. "Buddhist Hermeneutics," *Journal of the American Academy of Religion,* 46, no. 1 (1978).

Tucci, G. *On Some Aspects of the Doctrines of Maitreya (nātha) and Asaṅga.* Calcutta: University of Calcutta, 1930.

Ueda, Yoshifumi. "Two Main Streams of Thought in Yogācāra Philosophy." *Philosophy East and West,* 17 (January–October, 1967), 155–65.

Ui, H. "Maitreya as a Historical Personage," in *Indian Studies in Honor of Charles Rockwell Lanman.* Cambridge: Harvard University Press, 1929.

Warder, A. K. *Indian Buddhism.* Delhi: Motilal Banarsidass, 1970.

Warren, Henry Clarke. *Buddhism in Translations.* Cambridge: Harvard University Press, 1896. Rpt., New York: Atheneum, 1963.

Wayman, Alex. "Buddhism," in *Historia Religionum,* vol. II, *Religions of the Present.* Leiden: E. J. Brill, 1971.

—— "The Buddhism and the Sanskrit of Buddhist Hybrid Sanskrit." *Journal of the American Oriental Society,* 85, no. 1 (1965), 111–15.

—— "The Meanings of the Term Cittamātra." Paper delivered at the Association of Asian Studies Meeting, 1972.

—— "Nescience and Insight According to Asaṅga's *Yogācārabhūmi.*" Unpublished manuscript.

SELECTED BIBLIOGRAPHY

—— "The Yogācāra Idealism" (review article), *Philosophy East and West,* 15, no. 1 (1965), 65–73.

White, Nicholas P. "Aristotle on Sameness and Oneness," *The Philosophical Review,* 80, no. 2 (1971), 177–97.

Winternitz, Moriz. *A History of Indian Literature.* Vol. II. Translated by S. Ketkar and H. Kohn. Calcutta: University of Calcutta, 1927–33. Rpt., Delhi: Motilal Banarsidass, 1963.

Wittgenstein, Ludwig. *The Blue and Brown Books.* New York: Harper Torchbooks, 1965.

—— *Notebooks, 1914–1916.* Translated by G. E. M. Anscombe. New York: Harper Torchbooks, 1969.

—— *Philosophical Investigations.* Translated by G. E. M. Anscombe. New York: Macmillan, 1968.

—— *Tractatus Logico-Philosophicus.* Translated by D. F. Pears and B. F. McGuinness. London: Routledge and Kegan Paul, 1976.

Yamakami, Sogen. *Systems of Buddhistic Thought.* Calcutta: University of Calcutta, 1912.

Yampolsky, Philip B. *The Platform Sūtra of the Sixth Patriarch.* New York: Columbia University Press, 1967.

Zeyst, H. G. A. "Abhiññā," in *Encyclopaedia of Buddhism.* Vol. I, part I. Colombo: The Government Press, 1961.

Zimmer, Heinrich. *Philosophies of India.* Bollingen series, no. 26. London: Routledge and Kegan Paul, 1951.